21 MUGSHOTS

THE CONVERSION OF A CONVICT

BY BRITTNEY SINGLETON

21 Mugshots: The Conversion of a Convict

Trilogy Christian Publishers

A Wholly Owned Subsidiary of Trinity Broadcasting Network

2442 Michelle Drive, Tustin, CA 92780

Copyright © 2024 by Brittney Singleton

Scripture quotations marked ESV are taken from the ESV® Bible (The Holy Bible, English Standard Version®), copyright © 2001 by Crossway Bibles, a publishing ministry of Good News Publishers. Used by permission. All rights reserved. Scripture quotations marked GNT are taken from the Good News Translation® (Today's English Version, Second Edition). Copyright © 1982 American Bible Society. All rights reserved. Scripture quotations marked NIV are taken from the Holy Bible, New International Version®, NIV®. Copyright © 1973, 1978, 1984, 2011 by Biblica, Inc.TM Used by permission of Zondervan. All rights reserved worldwide. www.zondervan.com. The "NIV" and "New International Version" are trademarks registered in the United States Patent and Trademark Office by Biblica, Inc.TM Scripture quotations marked NKJV are taken from the New King James Version®. Copyright © 1982 by Thomas Nelson. Used by permission. All rights reserved. Scripture quotations marked TLB are taken from The Living Bible copyright © 1971. Used by permission of Tyndale House Publishers, a Division of Tyndale House Ministries, Carol Stream, Illinois 60188. All rights reserved.

All rights reserved, including the right to reproduce this book or portions thereof in any form whatsoever.

For information, address Trilogy Christian Publishing Rights Department, 2442 Michelle Drive, Tustin, Ca 92780.

Trilogy Christian Publishing/ TBN and colophon are trademarks of Trinity Broadcasting Network.

For information about special discounts for bulk purchases, please contact Trilogy Christian Publishing.

Trilogy Disclaimer: The views and content expressed in this book are those of the author and may not necessarily reflect the views and doctrine of Trilogy Christian Publishing or the Trinity Broadcasting Network.

10 9 8 7 6 5 4 3 2 1

Library of Congress Cataloging-in-Publication Data is available.

ISBN 979-8-89333-253-7

ISBN 979-8-89333-254-4 (ebook)

Dedication

I dedicate this book to Jesus first and foremost. I pray that He supernaturally uses it to touch even the hardest of hearts and plant a seed that one day will grow. In 1 Corinthians 3:6 (NIV) it says, "I planted the seed, Apollos watered it, but God has been making it grow." The person who plants and waters the seed is not important, but it is God who is important because He makes the seed grow. That is my prayer for this book—it may plant a seed, or it may water a seed that has already been planted, but I ask God to cause that seed to grow.

To my loving husband, Mitch, our love story is miraculous. God took two very broken people in Texas and somehow networked them into each other's lives in a beautiful and supernatural way. You listened to me; you waited on me. You were my best friend until the day you were my husband, and I thank you for that. Thank you for honoring me; thank you for encouraging me to write this book and telling me all the time how amazing I am. Thank you for being my biggest fan and always cheering me on. I love you. There have been many nights where I stayed late with a Bible and books in my hands, praying for and mentoring people, and my sweet husband would keep up with all my things and let me minister and not lose everything I carried into the meeting.

To my amazing children. Madisyn, Maci, Connor, and Maverick, the fantastic four. I will never give up on you, and I will always fight for you. My children were so hurt by my addiction, but they found it in their hearts to forgive me and let me back into their hearts and lives. Mitch and the kids are the second-best thing that ever happened to me, and they each changed my life in their own special way. I am so grateful God has allowed me to have such a wonderful core family. To Judah, my sweet grandson, my prayer for you is you always praise the Lord just like your name means. Genesis 29:35 (TLB), "Once again she was pregnant and had a son and named him Judah (meaning 'Praise'), for she said, 'Now I will praise Jehovah!' And then she stopped having children."

My father passed away in October of 2020. He got to see me filled with the Holy Spirit and radically different, and he always told me to go on TBN and give my testimony. God gave me seven beautiful years of restoration with my father before he went to the place Jesus prepared for him. I want to also dedicate this book to him. He always believed in me, he never gave up on me, and I am so proud to be his daughter. I had him programmed in my phone as "the greatest dad of all time," and he really was. I cannot wait to celebrate Jesus with him one day in heaven. When I was addicted, I wanted so badly to make my dad proud. Isn't it funny how in all of our human nature is a desire to please our father and make him proud? I would be strung out on drugs and tell my dad, "I am going to make you proud one day…" The last birthday card my father gave me read as follows, "Brittney, you always said you would make me proud, and you have. Your song is the sweetest…" I pray this book be a song that I sing to you, and I pray it is sweet to your ears and healing to your soul.

To my mother as well, she is so full of faith, and I don't think I would be the woman I am today without her influence in my life and without her prayers. She is living proof that you should never stop praying and believing for your children. She believed God would bring me back, and she didn't give up for eleven years. What if she had given up on the tenth year? You just never know when you are going to get your miracle! Do not ever give up praying for your children. Praying seems like the most insignificant thing you can do for an individual, but it is the most powerful thing you can do for an individual. God is the only One who can change the human heart, so why not plead to Him and ask Him to do it? You can ask for His strength in your weakness, and you can count on every promise in the Bible that He has for you and for your children. I would also like to dedicate it to the ones who have passed away over the years: Dustin Duncan, Miranda Streed, Lindsay Moore, and many other saints who have gone before us. These three whom I mentioned were all Christians, and I have a hope in my heart that I will see them again, and I pray that each of their personal stories will inspire you and encourage you to make the changes you need to make *now*. The Bible says "*now*" is the time; *now* is the time for salvation. Do not wait another minute to change; do not wait another minute to cry out to Jesus. Tomorrow is never promised, and we must learn that not everyone's story ends with a redemption that can be seen on earth. Some end with a redemption by the Holy Spirit in heaven, but do not let that be your story. If you have breath in your lungs, you have a chance to turn it all around, and you have a purpose and a destiny waiting for you.

Acknowledgments

I would like to thank the one person who made this dream happen for me: Trey Patterson. I met Trey years ago, and he became my boss. It was a risky move hiring a girl with my kind of past, but I remember him saying that my story inspired him and he wanted someone like me on his team. He owns several car dealerships across the region, and he is the greatest Christian man I know. He exemplifies Jesus in all that he does. He not only hired me to work for him, but he has been a friend and a mentor to me over the years. I have seen Trey help more people than can be counted. I have seen him sow into ministry after ministry without asking any questions. I want to be like Trey when I grow up. To Trey, thank you for supporting me, thank you for your yes to Jesus, and thank you for hiring me and seeing Jesus in me. Thank you for making this book happen.

Table of Contents

Preface..13
Chapter 1: Born on a Monday..................................15
Chapter 2: 2003, the Year of Glory..........................23
Chapter 3: The Heart...33
Chapter 4: Breaking Point.......................................41
Chapter 5: High Cost to Low Living........................47
Chapter 6: Big Girl Time-Out..................................57
Chapter 7: Halfway Home but Never Made It........65
Chapter 8: When Havin' a Cell Goes Wrong...........71
Chapter 9: Twin Time..77
Chapter 10: It's a Slow Fade When You Give Yourself Away.....89
Chapter 11: Betrayal..99
Chapter 12: Highway to Hell.................................107
Chapter 13: Demons..113
Chapter 14: Angels...125
Chapter 15: Chasing Rebels...................................137
Chapter 16: Bad News Comes First.......................151
Chapter 17: The Waiting..157
Chapter 18: Freedom...163
Chapter 19: You Gotta Start Somewhere..............167
Chapter 20: Go and Tell the Others.......................173
Chapter 21: Jesus over Everything........................185
About the Author..193

Preface

I was sitting on a hill in Hot Springs, Arkansas. The pen I was holding in my hand was a gift from Hettie Lue Brooks; she had given all the girls this pen as a gift over the weekend at the women's retreat I was at. Jesus had recently set me completely free, and I was on fire for God. His love had broken every chain of addiction, and I was a walking, talking miracle. I surrendered to His plan for me. I was so aware that the Holy Spirit had made His home inside of me. God was in me, and He was speaking to me and leading me into all truth. As I sat on that hill, I heard the Holy Spirit say, "Look up at the stars and tell Me what you see." I was so in awe of the Lord, lost in the wonder of His majesty, there was no telling what I was going to see when I looked up at those stars, so I tried to live in the moment and look up slowly with open eyes to see what He was showing me, an open heart to know what He was about to tell me. The pen in my hand was the shape of a diamond at the end, a huge jewel to show us girls our worth, how we are precious like a diamond and the pressures of life only make us more beautiful. When I looked up in the sky, I saw the stars in the shape of the pen I was holding in my hand, and I heard the Holy Spirit say so clearly, "I want you to write a book, Brittney...it will be twenty-one chapters, with twenty-one mug shots, and it will be a story of your life, but it will be used for My glory." That is where the vision was born in my heart, and that is how this book came into being. God gave me the vision out on that hill, and now you hold the very book He gave me a vision about. This book contains mug shots as proof of my depravity, proof of how far I was, how dead in my sin, but Christ died for me, the ungodly. While I was yet in my sin, in every mug shot is a picture of a girl that God chose to die for in that state I was in. What kind of love is that? What kind of grace? It is a supernatural, extraordinary kind of love. A love that defies scientific understanding and the laws of nature. Praise God for this kind of love. The only love that had the power to rescue me.

Chapter 1

BORN ON A MONDAY

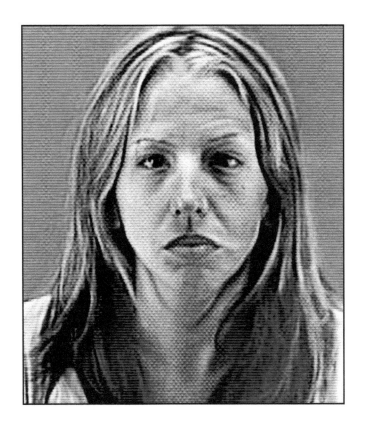

"For nothing will be impossible with God."

Luke 1:37 (ESV)

I was born on a Monday. Most people hate Mondays, but I have always loved this day of the week. I spent a *lot* of time in jail. I have been arrested twenty-one times. I know, I know, who in the world does not learn their lesson after the first time? Or the second? Or the third or fourth? Or the twentieth? Well, I guess me. A stubborn, hard heart is not easily bent and molded and changed. To this day, I am in *awe* of God being able to change the human heart; that is such a miracle.

When you are in jail, the weekends go by slowly, and when Monday finally gets there, you find out so much; you get mail again, and you find out when court dates are. It is sort of a fresh start to the week. You can breathe again because everything in the world starts having structure and order.

The Lord knows I love being able to start over. The Lord knew I needed some sort of structure and order. God knew that about me. Fun fact: all three of my children were born on Mondays. When my husband and I first started courting…I remember saying, "God, if he is the one, he will be born on a Monday…" Sure enough, he was! I want you to know that God knows you. He knows every part of you inside and out. He was there the first time you spoke your first words. He was there the first time you ever cried. He was there when you rode your bike for the first time. He was there when you fell and scraped your knee. He was there when you felt rejected and abandoned at your school. He has been there all along. You and God have history; you go way back, since even before He created the world. He knew you. He knows every detail of you. He is writing your story. He is the author, and you are His best novel. He is the artist, and you are His canvas. He is the architect; you are His blueprint. Only God can organize such wonderful and beautiful and intricate details. He is so complex. He is so marvelous. Knowing Him is beyond anything that you could ever imagine...I encourage you right now to trust Him. I am so glad my book made it into your hands. I have made a commitment to pray for each person who holds this book in their hand. You are not holding it by chance or by "accident." God put it right there in your hand, and He wants to speak to you through it. He brings hope to the hopeless. Maybe you are facing an impossible situation. He wants you to know that nothing is impossible with Him. No matter how big the mountain, that mountain can be moved. "For nothing will be impossible with God" (Luke 1:37, ESV). I want you to just think about that for a second, close your eyes, and meditate on it. Give God ten seconds to acknowledge Him and that He can do the impossible! I, too, was facing an impossible situation. I had lost all hope. I was a disappointment to my family. I was disappointed in myself. I was just a big fat disappointment walking around. I was a hopeless case, and I felt worthless. Oh, but Jesus. Jesus changes everything, doesn't He? Years ago, if you had told me that I was going to come out of addiction and prison and live for the Lord, I would have called you a liar. He turned everything around, though. Isn't that just like grace? Isn't that a perfect picture of Jesus? Jesus is a Savior to the drowning, and some of us are drowning. Can you imagine being in the middle of the ocean and knowing there is no way out and the impending feeling of death and doom creeping into your heart and seeing a hand stretch out toward you and offer you help? Jesus stretches out His hand to you right now, and He offers you a way out of the way you are living. He rescues you; He literally gives you another chance at life, and the best part is His mercies are new every morning. I certainly was not living for the Lord. I was strung out on drugs 60 percent of the time, but He chose me. John 15:16 (NIV), "You did not choose Me, but I chose you."

    I didn't choose Him. He chose me. And maybe that is enough to bring you hope right there. Ha! You don't choose God. He chooses you! He chose to die for you; He chose to pay the penalty for you; He chose you because His desire is to live in you. Jesus wants you; He sees you as valuable. He chose for this book to be in your hand and these words to be entering your mind at this very moment. It does not matter what state of mind you are in right now. It doesn't matter if you have cleaned up your life, if you got rid of that secret sin, if you have money or popularity; He chose you, and He still chooses you. So you can relinquish all control. You can truly let go of your life. Letting go is hard, but I encourage you to do it. I often use an illustration when mentoring people. I tell them to imagine they are on top of a 1000-foot building, and Jesus is at the bottom, and He is saying, "Come on. Jump." I encourage you to close your eyes and step forward and free fall, feel the wind in your hair as you fall, and trust, and I *promise* He will catch you. You can trust Him with your life and with your faith. You can trust Him in every single area of your life. When you lay down your life, *that* is when you find it. I did not start living until I relinquished control of my life. I laid my life down, and I died in a jail cell, and immediately after that I began to live. It truly is a beautiful exchange. My filth for His righteousness. My junk for His perfection. My shame for His glory. Speaking of that old stinky jail cell, I would like to tell you about my life. I would like to tell you about the twenty-one times I was arrested...I would like to tell you about the moment that Christ came in through the door of my heart and changed the trajectory of my entire life...

I was born on Monday, May 20th, 1985. I was a rebellious kid by nature. We are born selfish. If you don't believe me, give any two random toddlers one toy and see what happens. They will shout out that magic word "mine," and, buddy, you better back off. I was born to be a bit of a rule breaker, and it didn't help much that I was spoiled rotten. My mom had a hard time telling me no. I ran the show for most of my life. I was extremely strong-willed and hardheaded, and I did not do well when things did not go my way. My mom was a saint.

She did all the right things. I like to joke around that I had a "drug" problem before I had a "drug" problem because she "*drug*" my hiney to church. When I was younger, every Sunday, I watched my mother worship the Lord passionately. My mom is a radical worshiper; she is a radical woman in general! She, too, was a broken girl, molested by a family member…praise God for one of her high school teachers knowing the Lord and leading her to Jesus. When my mom got saved, my mom got *saved*; she was all in for Jesus. She went to church every time the doors opened. I remember watching her go to the front of the church and *pour* out her praise on the Lord. I wanted to be just like her when I grew up. She would pour out her praise on Jesus; she would worship Him with her hands held high. She was on the dance team in our church, so oftentimes she would wear long, beautiful dresses that made her look like an angel as she was dancing. My mother was the most beautiful woman in the world to me. I was so scared to do anything like lift my hands or dance. I would think, *I hope I am brave enough to be like her one day.* I literally remember being about nine years old and wanting what she had but also being scared to be bold like she was. In Matthew, Mark, and Luke, there is a story about a woman who came into a house where Jesus was and poured out expensive oil on him. The Bible says, "A woman…who lived a sinful life" (Luke 7:37, NIV), and she wasted thousands of dollars on the head of Jesus. It was a radical move, but she didn't care what anybody thought. She broke the normal that day. She broke the jar, but she also broke her pride; she broke the power her sinful life had over her, and she wasted all of it on Him. The Bible says that "surely wherever the gospel is preached in the whole world, what she had done will be told in memory of her" (Matthew 26:13, NIV). My mom reminded me a lot of the woman who poured out the expensive perfume on Jesus. She gave Him everything; she honored God, and God, in return, honored her. She would stand on faith and make us read the Bible on the way to school. She would buy us all the latest

'90s Christian music that came out. DC Talk, Petra, and Carmen. Back in the '90s, Christian music was not nearly as cool as it is today. Today, if you are a believer, there is no excuse; they have every type of music you can think of. Back then, not so much, and it wasn't cool at all to listen to that stuff, but I didn't have much of a choice. We would fight every day on the way to school over the radio. She would flip it to Christian, and I would flip it to secular. She was strong in faith, but I was very strong-willed and did not back down easily. Some days she would win that battle, and some days I would, but she always let me know that secular music was no good for me. She would say, "Brittney, garbage in, garbage out." I would just try to manipulate her and make her think my kind of music "wasn't that bad" and some of it had "spiritual lyrics," and she should really listen to my kind and give it a try and quit being so single-minded in her opinions and views.

My mother attended women's retreats in Hot Springs, Arkansas, when I was a young girl. She would leave on Friday and come back changed on Sunday. I would get excited when she left because I knew the Lord would touch her at those retreats. She would come back being nice. When I was old enough, she sent me to the kids' camp they had, it was called Brookhill Ranch. I got saved when I was thirteen at that summer camp. It was the summer of 1998, and they did a play about the crucifixion. All the counselors were dressed like Roman soldiers and disciples, and, of course, Jesus; that play wrecked me. As I sat on the hill that hot summer night, I looked over my left shoulder, and I saw these flames coming up the hill. It looked like a Roman soldier holding these thick sticks that were on fire at the end, sort of like a giant match. The Roman soldiers beat Jesus, and it looked so real, and He had blood dripping down His body, and there were women following Him, wailing and crying. The closer they got, the more it pierced my heart. As they brought Jesus up that hill, I realized that this story really happened. This was not a fairy tale; this is what Jesus really did, and in a way, it made the Bible come alive to me, and I was caught up in the story. The hardest part was listening to the hammer hit that old wooden cross. They drove the nails in his hands and feet with a loud bang against that old, rugged cross, and I gave my life to Jesus that hot summer night. They asked if anyone wanted to know Jesus, if anyone was impacted by that night. I was brave like my mom, and I walked up to that cross, and I gave my life to Jesus. After all, look at what He did for me. The pain, the blood, the torture. That night impacted me.

In Ephesians 1:13–14 (NKJV) it says:

> *In Him you also trusted, after you heard the word of truth, the gospel of your salvation; in whom also, having believed, you were sealed with the Holy Spirit of promise, who is the guarantee of our inheritance until the redemption of the purchased possession, to the praise of His glory.*

Many years later the Lord would show me this very night. He took me to that night and showed me my little thirteen-year-old self in the Spirit, and as I walked up to the cross, He showed me that was when I was marked and sealed for the day of redemption, just like the Bible says. I saw heaven mark me. Heaven marked me with a white light on my forehead, and I became Christ's possession that night, sealed by His Spirit. I wish I could say that is the end of the story, but it is not. Unfortunately, I would have a lot of dark days ahead of me. That day is probably the actual day that hell put an assignment against me and my life. The devil tried so hard to keep me from the purpose God created for me. I think hell knew if I got a hold of Jesus, there would be many lives impacted by it. So, after that day, the real tests of my heart started coming…and just as quickly as that fire started in me, the fire started fading. I went right back to listening to that secular music that was no good for me. I went right back to flesh and music and boys and popularity.

Chapter 2

2003, THE YEAR OF GLORY

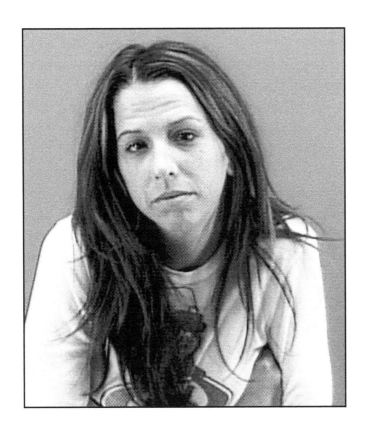

> *"Before I formed you in the womb, I knew you, and before you were born, I consecrated you; I appointed you a prophet to the nations."*
>
> Jeremiah 1:5 (ESV)

This is one of my favorite scriptures. It teaches us that nothing happens by accident, not even teen pregnancy. It is planned...just not so much by the teenager. There is a heavenly agenda and a heavenly purpose going on and we must learn how to see it with our spiritual eyes. We must learn to not shun or judge when these situations arise. We must learn how to have the heart of God. We must learn to look at that unborn child as a prophet to the nations known and appointed by God Himself. Let's just ask God to help us see things differently right now. Let's invite Him to give us heavenly eyes. Let's invite Him into the last place we felt disappointed and invite Him to show us how He sees it. I encourage you to never be disappointed in the Lord. Disappointment is the biggest killer of faith. Satan uses disappointment to destroy our faith, and God uses disappointment to build our faith! In John 11:32 (ESV) it says, "Then, when Mary came where Jesus was, and saw Him, she fell at his feet, saying to Him, 'Lord, if you had been here, my brother would not have died.'" Mary was disappointed that Jesus was not there when Lazarus died, but heaven had a resurrection planned! Jesus ended up raising Lazarus from the dead! Sometimes, when things don't go our way, we think to ourselves, *God, if You had been here, this wouldn't have happened*, but I challenge you to look for the resurrection in your situation. Try your best to trust that God does everything He does on purpose. There is purpose in the pain, but there is indeed pain.

In 2003 I was a senior at East Texas Christian High School. My parents were devout believers, so I felt like I had been in Christian School since I was born. If there was such a thing as a Christian School for newborn babies, I would have been enrolled. By the time

I was a senior, I had been a Christian for five years. I remember being very curious about drugs this year. In high school I struggled badly with insecurity. I felt stupid. I felt ugly. I felt worthless and unseen. It wasn't because my family didn't love me. It was because by the time I was a teenager I was already starting to believe the lies of the enemy. I wanted so badly to be loved and accepted, but for whatever reason I felt rejected. These feelings led me to do things. I wanted to fill the void inside with whatever numbed me and made me feel different in the moment. I wanted to feel confident, and I wanted to feel pretty, so I would drink because I felt confident when I drank. I would feel pretty when I looked in the mirror after drinking. By the time I was fifteen, I had already experimented with sex. I lied a lot. I lied to my parents. I was constantly telling them that I was out doing something that involved Jesus or church, but I really wasn't. Most of the time, I was drinking or smoking pot with my friends. I would go to chapel every day at my private Christian school, and sometimes I would even lead the prayer or help with the devotional or chapel setup, but my heart was far from the Lord. My flesh was winning most of the battle. I was a good kid; my family and friends loved me and looked up to me, but I was also deeply insecure and was craving love and attention.

I met Gabriel when I was seventeen. Gabriel was so very handsome, and I fell in love with him very quickly. I could not believe that he was into me; he was older than me and way out of my league. He was the most good-looking man I had ever seen; I was very impressed by the way he dressed. He always ironed his shirts, and he wore nice hats and clothes. He was known for dating older women, and here I was, still in high school, and he was interested in me. I was out with a girlfriend not long after I met him, and someone introduced us to a new drug that had just started becoming popular. The street name for the drug was "X," short for "ecstasy." I remember thinking of it as like a vitamin; you just take one, and it makes you feel good, so it couldn't be that bad for you. I justified it in my mind that way and thought, *I won't get addicted. I am a smart girl.* I will never forget the first night I tried this drug. I was instantly in a heavenly state. I was *obsessed* with how this drug made me feel. I went into the night having problems at home and major self-esteem issues, and by the time the night ended, I felt confident about myself and all my problems had gone away, and I was happy. I had not been happy at all when the night started; that is why we drank. We weren't happy with ourselves, and we didn't think highly of ourselves at all, so we would try to fill that hole inside by drinking and making ourselves "feel" different. The first night I took it, Gabriel and his friends had taken some as well, and we all ended up at the same place. That night, Gabriel came over to me and said, "You are the most beautiful girl I have ever seen…inside and out…" I knew that I had found my soulmate and that I wanted to be with Gabriel for the rest of my life. Our relationship got serious quickly. I would find myself going to meet him every day. We smoked a lot of pot, and we would meet up to smoke before and after school. Sometimes I would skip school to be with Gabriel. Boy, we were in love. One night, when we were "rolling" (under the influence of ecstasy), I had a weird feeling. Something was not right. We had been having unprotected sex, and that night I felt strange about taking and doing the drugs we had always done. I went to the store with my girlfriend, and we got a pregnancy test. When we got back to the house, I peed on the stick, and sure enough, I was pregnant. This was the beginning of 2003. I was scheduled to graduate from East Texas Christian School that May. I was also the salutatorian of my class. I don't know how, but somehow, I managed to get good grades during school. So here I was, pregnant, and the first thought that came to my mind was, *I need to get married.* Gabriel had already given me a promise ring for Christmas, so I knew in my heart that he would marry me and take care of me and this baby.

My pregnancy almost killed me. I was so sick. I was sick every morning. I knew that I was going to have to tell my parents soon because they would notice me puking every time I woke up or ate or drove or anything. I took my mom to lunch to tell her. We sat at a little booth at McAlister's Deli, and I said, "Mom, I have to tell you something." She just smiled and asked, "Okay, what?" I told her, "Mom, I'm pregnant." My mom was so full of grace and full of mercy. She loved me no matter what. She is such a picture of Jesus. She started crying and asked me once, "Are you serious?" I told her, "Yes, I am serious." She asked me what we were going to do. I told her we wanted to get married before I graduated high school. We wanted to get married before anyone else found out.

March 29th, 2003, Gabriel and I got married. My dad was furious. He chased Gabriel out of our house when we told him. He was not going to accept it at all. He was so disappointed in me. He even told me when I got pregnant, "Brittney, you have placed a knife in my back, and we will never be okay again." That really hurt because up until I got pregnant my father and I were very close. I never let anyone get in between my father and me until I met Gabriel. I was daddy's girl. My dad had a little bit of an anger problem, though, so when he was mad, I knew it. Disappointing my dad was almost the end of me. Being pregnant as a teenager, out of wedlock, was hard enough, but living with my dad during all of this was terrible. He was very close to stopping me from getting married, but that strong-willed little girl once again won a battle she should never have won. I had such bad jitters on the day I got married. I smoked weed right before I walked down the aisle. I was seventeen; I was a little girl. I had no idea how to be an adult. Up to this point, my parents had done everything for me. And here I was, pretending like I grew up at a wedding with my peers. I had to be back at school that Monday. I still can't believe I got married. It just all seems so crazy to me now. How could my parents not tell me that this would be a dreadful mistake? How could they give me away that day? Knowing I was so immature? And just a little girl? I had no idea what I was doing, but I sure acted like I did.

I was so confident that was what I wanted, and I was so stubborn. Like I mentioned before, a stubborn and hard heart is not easily bent and molded. My heart was so set on being married to Gabriel, and the baby growing inside my belly sealed the deal. There was no way I was not getting married; it was over and a done deal in my mind.

We got married, and I went back to school that Monday. Rumors were starting to go around school. It was obvious I was throwing up every few minutes. I remember I told a few of my very trusted teachers, and it wasn't long until I got called to the principal's office. The principal just pretty much asked me point blank, and I admitted that, yes, I was pregnant, and that was why I got married. The principal told me that she would have to take it in front of the school board and see what they wanted to do. The principal was like my mom; she was full of grace and mercy, and I currently go to church with her. She really fought for me during all of this. She was my English teacher in tenth grade, so she and I had a bond, and she secretly was my favorite teacher. She was the best, and I still love her to this day. She had a meeting with the school board, and they let me know that I could not go to school there anymore. I would not be able to return after that day. That was a big disappointment. I had worked hard at that school since I was in the tenth grade. I was sad to leave. I went to an alternative school and ended up getting my diploma from them… But it just wasn't the same.

I was dealing with a lot of shame from being pregnant and married at such a young age. Gabriel and I had managed to get our own place with me working at a tanning salon and him working for his dad. It was a duplex, but it worked for us.

At home, Gabriel started hurting me. We would get into fights, and he would grab me and start choking me. Even though I was pregnant with his baby and we were married, he was very violent. Gabriel was also not ready to be a husband or a dad. He was not saved and had no idea how to lead me. I had to let go of the drugs because I was pregnant, but he did not want to. He kept partying and doing drugs, and eventually we would fight, and he would hurt me. It was a nightmare. I didn't do anything to deserve this. I was living a nightmare. He was messing my mind up so badly telling me how ugly I was and how I would be fat after I had our baby. He would disappear and not come home at night, and I would find out he was with other women. I would cry so much over Gabriel. I would just sit at home and cry at the terrible choice I had made by leaving my dad and marrying this man who was hurting me and cheating on me. Those were some dark days.

I did have one hope through it all, though. The sweet baby that I was carrying.

I would hold my tummy and sing to her. I would tell her I was sorry when Gabriel was yelling at the top of his lungs at me. Looking back, I realize the physical abuse was very traumatic for me. I came out of a Christian home where there was no abuse. I entered one of the most abusive, toxic relationships I had ever been in. Maybe that is part of why I went as far in as I did with sin and drugs. I was a very broken girl. The baby girl living inside of me was the only thing that kept me going. He would break me down, but he wouldn't break her down; he couldn't because she was abiding in me, and he couldn't hurt her. I wanted to give my baby a good life. I wanted her to have a mom and a dad. I wanted to fix myself for her. She was worth it; even if I had messed up my life, I could still help her.

September 29th, 2003, my life changed for the better. I gave birth to a beautiful baby girl. I named her Madisyn. Madisyn really opened my eyes to life. I loved her so much. She was everything to me. I remember the night I brought her home she cried and cried. I was covered in teetee, and there were diapers all over the place. My house was a wreck, and I called my mom crying. I asked her to please come over and help me, and she did. I have never slept so well in my life. I needed it. I had been up since I gave birth pretty much. And that is what you do when you become a mommy. But I was so used to sleeping at my parents' house that this new mommy thing was tough. Gabriel wasn't making enough money to pay our bills, and we were always having to borrow money from both sides of our family. The abuse did not go away. Matter of fact, after I had Madisyn, it got worse. There were several nights that Gabriel would get twisted off on drugs and get violent, even with the baby in the house. We had holes in our walls from him slamming me around and getting so angry that he would punch the wall. I got to a point where I would just hide. I would hide from family and friends; I could not invite anyone over because I did not want them to see the wreckage of my life. Gabriel had a friend that would save me from his violent attacks, and I ended up becoming romantically involved with him. He was a safe place for me, but he was Gabriel's best friend. I knew how wrong it was, but Gabriel had broken me down so much, I didn't care anymore—at least this man was nice to me, and he wouldn't hurt me. So I found myself in a situation where I was cheating on my husband with his best friend.

I had to get out, so I filed for divorce and left Gabriel. When I left, Gabriel really started losing his mind. I remember he called my parents' house phone ninety-nine times one day. He would just call and call and call. I was honestly scared of him. He told me he would kill me, and I believed him. I had been hurt by him physically so many times that I knew he had it in him to take my life. As a matter of fact, he had choked me so many times that I thought I might die. I will never forget the phone call I received one spring morning that said, "Brittney, are you sitting down?" I responded, "Yes, why?" The person on the other end told me, "Gabriel has shot himself. He is alive, but an ambulance just picked him up. He shot himself in the hand." By the time I got to the hospital, the damage had been done. Gabriel had an X-ray of his hand, and that little pinky finger was shattered. I will never forget when he shot himself in the hand, he had a shirt on that said, "I lie to girls." I remember thinking, *Maybe you shouldn't do that anymore considering...*

The doctor came in and asked if I was his wife and told me they were going to have to amputate his little finger and part of his hand. It was awful, but in a way, it woke me up. I realized that Gabriel was no longer a safe place, and with how violent and crazy he was and the fact he had guns and the fact he shot himself was all too much. He could shoot me and probably not think twice about it...or even worse, Madisyn. What if he hurt Madisyn? There was no way I was going to stick around and find out...

Chapter 3

THE HEART

"The heart is deceitful above all things and beyond cure. Who can understand it?"

Jeremiah 17:9 (NIV)

Our hearts are wicked, aren't they? I believe this scripture is talking about the heart before it comes to the Lord. I would even argue that when we run from the Lord and the plans He has for us... our hearts grow more and more wicked and hard. A hard heart is a wicked heart. A hard heart has made up its mind to not let anyone in and to do things itself. Can we take a moment and place our hands over our heart? Can we ask the Lord to soften us? I want you to close your eyes and picture a real soft heart pillow...now I want you to squeeze that pillow and feel how soft it is. Let's ask the Lord to make our hearts soft like that again. Let's invite Him to soften us. We get so hard, and we get so critical and nasty. Lord God, would You soften our hearts right now? I often ask the Lord to soften my heart; life has a way of hardening us. A soft heart is easy to rend. To rend means to tear open. God tells us to rend our hearts, not our garments. In the Old Testament, when the chosen ones of the Lord would go through heartache, they would tear their clothes in the presence of the Lord as an outward expression of their hearts being broken before the Lord, but the Lord wants us to rend our hearts, He is not interested in the outward appearance but the inward. We don't have to physically tear our clothes if we just inwardly tear our hearts open before him. We must fling wide the doors of our chest and let God in.

Leaving Gabriel was hard. Most of the time, leaving a toxic relationship must be planned out in your head and tried repeatedly before it becomes a reality. I applied for an apartment at Longview Square Apartments after I left him. I stayed with my parents while I was waiting for a government apartment to become available. The whole time my parents were begging me to just stay with them. But no… I was grown up and I had to have my own way. I was never very good at following rules anyway. The waiting list at Longview Square was something crazy like three years, but it did not take that long at all. I think I got into my apartment within six or seven months after applying. Madisyn was a baby. Between my parents and my ex-in-laws, someone was always helping me with Madisyn. I was so selfish, and I still wanted to party and do my own thing. I already had a new love interest. Coming out of that abusive, toxic relationship hit my self-esteem hard. If a boy just thought I was pretty, then I thought that "he was the one." I was so desperate for someone to love me. For someone to truly accept me. For someone to look at me with a dove's eyes that would never want anyone else. Running from God and desperate for love is a bad combination. I ended up seeing my new love interest for the course of the next couple of years. He introduced me to pain pills, which was a whole new world.

After maybe five months at Longview Square, they did a routine check of all the apartments. They came into my apartment, and it smelled like marijuana and had male clothes in it. And just like that, I got kicked out as quickly as they let me in. Back to my parents' house I went. My love interest was gone a lot. He worked in the oil field and was out of town a lot. He only came into town ever so often, so I started trying to work things out with Gabriel. Gabriel had a friend that he bought weed from, and he would always take me over to the guy's house. We would go over to his house and hang out for hours. I liked that this man had his own place, a house, and I liked that he had a job.

Sullivan was a good ol' boy. He worked at a tire shop, and he would sell weed on the side to make ends meet. The first time Sullivan ever met me, I could tell he was in love. He played with Madisyn, and he looked at me as if he had to have me. Like he couldn't live without me. Sullivan and I ended up hanging out more and more, and eventually he asked Madisyn and me to move in. Before he did that, though, he talked to Gabriel. He told Gabriel, "Look, I am in love with her, and I want to be with her..." We were all drinking that night, and it made Gabriel furious. I can't remember how, but I do remember Gabriel hurting me very badly that night. I woke up with a huge burn on my arm, and I could not remember how it happened, but I knew Gabriel had something to do with it. I had taken some anxiety medicine that night, and when you drink on it, it basically wipes out your memory, but the last thing I remembered that night was Gabriel and I arguing really badly in the car. We were throwing punches at each other and screaming at each other, and I knew there had been a physical altercation between us. Then I woke up with a massive burn all the way down my arm like someone had burned me with a torch or something. When I asked Gabriel, he said it must have happened amid the fight we had, but he couldn't remember either because we were both under the influence of the same drugs. Gabriel hated Sullivan now in his heart. And this would just be the first of many bad mistakes to come. I moved in with Sullivan while still having my oil field, friendly love interest on the side. This was basically a love triangle. I had a baby with Gabriel, and I was married to him at one point, so he always had that place in my heart. I was falling in love with Sullivan, and he was working every day to provide for Madisyn. But I had Remy, my tall oil field guy, who would come into town every now and then and see me. It was all one big mess. This year in which all of this was going on would be the *first* out of twenty-one times I would get arrested.

On September 13th, 2005, I got arrested for no insurance and expired registration on my car. The police did not know this, but in 2005 I was starting to become heavily reliant on pain pills. And this instance, when I was getting arrested, I had a bottle of pain pills in the car that they never found. I called Sullivan when I got arrested, and he and Remy started getting the bond money together to get me out. I remember telling them on the phone that I had some pills in my 4 Runner, and they could have some if they would just come get me. I warned them not to take all of them, though. I fantasized about eating those pills the whole time I was in jail. I could not wait to get out and take them. There was a group of us who were starting to get deep into pain pills in Longview. One of my friends was Dustin Duncan, who I mentioned earlier in the dedication part of my book. Dustin was the coolest person you could ever meet. He had it all; he always drove the jacked-up trucks, and he raced cars, and he had the most beautiful girlfriend who loved him so much. He was a picture of everything I wanted. He had looks, popularity, and love. I wanted all of that. He was attractive and not just physically; you just wanted to be around him all the time. He had the best personality and style, but he did have a side that not a lot of people knew. He partied and drank, and somehow his morals started getting corrupted by the bad company he kept. I was part of that bad company sometimes. We hung out on the weekends sometimes, him and me and my brother and all our friends. Dustin had such a different life with his girlfriend and family that we didn't get to see him a lot, so when we did, we loved spending time with him and would try to pull all-nighters since he finally got to come out. We would go out and get his truck stuck in the mud for fun, and, boy, was it fun. He was also known for arm wrestling; one of the first things he would want to do when we would all be sitting around and drinking is arm wrestling. He would make me feel so special. He would say, "All right, Brittney, let's go…" and he would act like I was winning the arm wrestle and act like I was so strong, and then he would slam me right at the end when he had everyone tricked. I felt bad because I was friends with Dustin's girlfriend, and I would watch her cry a lot over Dustin while he would be out doing his thing. I would hang out with her on some weekends and tell her how sorry I was that she couldn't get a hold of him, and then I would hang out with him sometimes while she would be blowing up his phone looking for him, and he would ignore her. It was a mess. It got better over time, and he got better over time, and she married him.

He was the love of Abby's life. She was so crazy about him. He was the only boy she had ever loved since she was a teenager. Their wedding was beautiful, seeing God join them together after all the years of hell she went through, she got her man. I don't know what happened after they got married or where it all went wrong; we didn't hang out nearly as much as we did before he got married, but I am assuming that the drugs and alcohol that we used to do when we were younger got worse for Dustin, and on November 23rd, 2005, I got a phone call that Dustin had passed away. I was in total shock. There was no way that Dustin could die; he was invincible. He was the toughest guy I knew. I was broken, and not only me but my brother and all our friends. We all had Christian roots, so it made us start thinking about our own lives and our own eternities. It challenged us to stop using drugs and pills and to try somehow to get our lives together for our friend. We attended Dustin's funeral together. Remy, Sullivan, my brother, and myself. We watched his beautiful mother and father and sister and brother lay their precious family member to rest, and it shattered all our hearts. We were all going through withdrawals from pills because when we found out about Dustin, we said no more. After we left the funeral, tears were streaming down all our faces, and the only noise in the truck was the road noise. Remy wiped the tears off his face and said, "Okay, I cannot take this anymore. I am going to the liquor store." We were all relieved when he said it. We were all thinking about it; we just didn't want to say it. We all drank the pain away that night. We had no idea how to process Dustin's death without the Lord. All we knew was we were hurting, and we were miserable, and we wanted our friend back. We tried to stop the pills for him, but it only lasted three or four days because we didn't understand the power of the Holy Spirit.

The Bible says, "The heart is deceitful above all things and beyond cure. Who can understand it?" (Jeremiah 17:9, NIV). That is so true. My heart was wicked. Always wanting to take things that would numb the pain and take the pain away. You know, I have come to learn this one thing. Pain is a good thing. Sometimes we need to feel pain. Pain causes us to lean into the *only One* who can help us. The only One that can truly make the pain go away. Jesus is the only answer. He is our only hope.

Sullivan, Remy, and I all smoked cigarettes in the house. We drank every night and smoked all day every day. One day my parents came to pick up Madisyn, and my father was very stern with me. He looked at Madisyn coughing and sneezing and having a hard time breathing, and he said to me, "You can ruin your life if you want to, but you are not taking this little girl down with you." He told me that he was going to take Madisyn if I didn't straighten up. They would come to pick her up all the time because they wanted her to be in a better environment than what I had her in. The truth is I did not deserve Madisyn. I deserved to lose her. I was not a good mother, and the main reason is that I was broken, insecure, selfish, and all the things you do not want to be. I had her right in the middle of all my junk. Perhaps the hardest things to get past are the injustices on our children. The way I was toward Madisyn made me hate myself even more. I was literally the worst mother to her. I was mean and hateful to her and treated her like crap. I was nothing like a mother should be. Even in my sober state of mind, I did not know how to mother her, and because of not being able to treat her like she deserved made me hate myself more and more. Why could I not get it right for her? Why couldn't I be like my mother? What was wrong with me? The guilt and shame piled up higher and higher until it was a fortress that surrounded me; there was no getting past those walls. Who could knock them down? Certainly not any human hand or any human strength. It was going to take someone with superhuman power and strength to reach me.

Chapter 4

BREAKING POINT

"There is a way that appears to be right, but in the end, it leads to death."

Proverbs 14:12 (NIV)

I often tell people I mentor when tragedy strikes, you have a choice to make. Either you can choose to go further or deeper into sin, which most people do, or you can choose to ask Jesus to help you get back on track and to comfort you and to set you free from yourself. I chose to go further into sin, and the tragedy that struck my life this year was in the form of court papers.

I worked at Chili's during this time, and I was shacking up with another woman most of the time. I was in between my parents' house or Gabriel's mom's house or this little apartment beside Chili's. I was working, but I was stealing from Chili's. I was so crazy that I would change the tip amounts that people would leave me. I was in a terrible place in my mind and my heart. I was searching for love in all the wrong places. One night, after a long night at the bar, I heard a knock on my girlfriend's door. She went to get it and said there was a processor there for me. A nice, friendly-looking man with glasses said, "Are you Brittney Major?" "Yes, sir," I spoke. He handed me some papers, and the first thing I saw was "restraining order against Madisyn Major." I sat on those steps, frozen in pain, tears streaming down my face. I could not believe this. How could she? How in the world could she do something so heinous and hateful to me?

Gabriel's mom was taking me to court for Madisyn. She had seen the way I was living. Partying, drinking, and smoking and running around doing crazy things. And she had seen enough. She was taking me to court for full custody of Madisyn. As many of you know, going through a custody battle is not easy. As a matter of fact, custody battles are hard and ugly. Gabriel's mom had such hatred in her heart for me. I felt like she had always wanted to take Madisyn from me. I felt like that was her twisted, evil plan all along. She hated me. She had a reason to; I had cheated on her son with his best friend. Her son had recently shot himself in the hand and blamed it on me. We did not get along at all. She was very cunning. She would make me feel like she was my friend, and I would tell her all my struggles. She would tell me she could relate, and she was an addict/alcoholic as well, but she had taken all the stuff I told her in confidence, and she had used it against me in court. It was the first time I had experienced betrayal. My parents would tell me not to trust her, but I was so naïve, I would trust her anyway, and it ended up backfiring on me. I loved Madisyn more than anything. I did not want to lose her; I did not want to be the person I was. I was trapped. I did not see a way out. In my own strength, I just couldn't stop the things I was doing. I wanted to have Madisyn, but I just couldn't clean up my life, but I was going to try. So I did just that. I laid off the drugs and alcohol and cleaned up my life a bit. I was asked to take a hair follicle test, and I complied and went down to the drug testing facility, where they cut my hair to test it. We decided to settle things out of court and go to a "mediation" type facility. At this mediation, my parents and their attorney, me and my attorney, and the in-laws and their attorney all sat at a table and talked about what was going to be best for Madisyn. My parents really wanted us to live with them, but it was so hard to get along with my parents. We fought a lot because of the lifestyle I chose. My in-laws wanted Madisyn to live with them, and because they had filed the lawsuit, that is where Madisyn was. I will never forget this day. During the meeting my drug test results became available. Basically, if I passed the drug test, Madisyn would live with my parents and me. If I failed the drug test, I would lose her. The fax came in. My lawyer walked over and read them and sort of hung her head low. She said, "Brittney, you have tested positive for methamphetamine and marijuana." It was a victory for my in-laws. I was devastated. Up until then I had only done meth twice. I could *not* believe that it had somehow stayed in my system after such a long time. I began to wail. I was crying so hard and so loud. I was in absolute shock. I had just lost my baby. I had not seen her in fourteen days, and now who knew when I would see her again? The car ride home was pure hell. My mom and dad were so disappointed. That day, I dropped the identity of a caring, loving mother. I picked up the identity of a dope head. I let the tragedy of losing my baby push me in the absolute other direction of where I should be going. I was sick. I hated myself. I was such a stupid girl. I made up my mind then that if I had to live without Madisyn, I was not going to live at all. I was about to really throw my life away. Madisyn was the only thing that gave me hope. She was the only reason I had not given up. And now they were taking her from me. My dad did not know how to love me through this. We would end up getting in screaming matches, and I would end up leaving. I loved my daddy so much, and it mattered what he thought of me. When he was not happy with me, it killed me on the inside. My spiritual decline had a lot to do with the father wounds I received during this time. I was wounded deep in my soul by my dad saying some of the things he said to me. He was doing his best, but he was full of fear. He loved me so much that it was killing him to see me go down this road; his number one fear was Gabriel's mom getting custody of Madisyn. Gabriel's mom lived with another woman, and my dad wanted to be a dad to Madisyn. He would say, "That little girl needs a daddy," and he was right. To lose Madisyn that day was pretty much a death sentence in my parents' eyes. They had invested so much money in a lawyer so they could get custody of her, and they would have if I had just passed that drug test. This would have all been fine if not for me. I was the problem. I felt ashamed. I felt stupid. I felt betrayed. I felt hated. I felt so many negative emotions. This is when my life really started to go downhill. This was my breaking point. We all have breaking points; we let things build and build, and eventually we break. I saw an illustration once of a man blowing up a balloon. As he blew, he said, "You are the balloon, and the air entering it is stress and anxiety and the cares of life." The balloon kept getting bigger and bigger until it burst; that is what happens to us—eventually we burst. He took his two fingers and pulled apart the end of the balloon where he had been blowing air, and it made this awful whiny noise. He was letting the air out, and he said, "This is when we process our anxiety and stress with the Lord, and we probably sound like this too, whiny." His point was we must let the air out. We must process the things going on in our hearts, and what better way than to talk out loud to the Father? I love Matthew 6:6 (NIV); it says, "But when you pray, go into your room, close the door and pray to your Father, who is unseen. Then your Father, who sees what is done in secret, will reward you." It just really doesn't get any simpler than that! How do we handle stress and anxiety? Heartache and pain? We go to our room, and we shut the door, and we talk out loud to the Lord as if He is right there with us. After all, He is.

Chapter 5

HIGH COST TO LOW LIVING

> *Those who live according to the flesh have their minds set on what the flesh desires; but those who live in accordance with the Spirit have their minds set on what the Spirit desires. The mind governed by the flesh is death, but the mind governed by the Spirit is life and peace. The mind governed by the flesh is hostile to God; it does not submit to God's law, nor can it do so. Those who are in the realm of the flesh cannot please God.*
>
> Romans 8:5–8 (NIV)

There is a high cost to low living. If you want to continue to live in the world and continue to party, you will pay the price. Sin will take you further than you want to go and leave you there longer than you want to stay. The devil is not playing games. He dips lies into honey, and he makes them look delicious, and once you start messing around with him, he takes your life if he can. He is a liar; he is a murderer. He wants to destroy you.

After I lost Madisyn, I just didn't care. I would go to my local Walmart and steal makeup or CDs or clothes. I would steal whatever I wanted. I hated myself. I had a lying problem, and I was starting to develop a stealing problem. The stealing problem got so bad that Walmart put a criminal trespass order on me where I was not even allowed in the building. I walked in with my mom and our pastor's wife to get my nails done one day and sat down in the chair, and the lady started working on my nails, and here came the LPD, asked me to put my hands behind my back, and arrested me, right in front of my mom and my pastor's wife. That is how bad the stealing had been and how serious the criminal trespass was. I booked into jail that day with four-inch nails because the lady didn't get to cut them down or anything before they hauled me off the jail. I wanted what I wanted when I wanted it, and I didn't care who was in my way. I was going to get what I wanted. I was twenty-one years old in 2006, and I was pretty like my mama. I was never faithful in any relationship. I had attention problems. If you showed me attention, I would usually give myself away to you. I was deeply insecure and truly had no idea of my worth or my value. I could not hold down a job to save my life. I would always mess around and not show up or get fired. My dad was in the car business, and somehow, I ended up meeting another man in the car business. This man was a lot older than me, but he liked me. He was upfront with me and told me that I was a beautiful girl and that he could help a girl like me get on her feet and have some money and a car and a place to live. It would cost me, though. I didn't care; I was on the highway to hell anyway. I had lost Madisyn, and she was the only one who really meant anything to me, so I started seeing this man more and more. He introduced me to the idea that if you are a pretty girl, you can sleep with men, and they will take care of you financially. He was very coyly introducing me to prostitution. *What a great idea*, I thought. I would come over and sleep with him, and he would pay me. It started out innocently enough, and the shopping sprees we went on were my favorite. He would let me pick out anything in the store, and sometimes he would let me bring a friend, and she could pick out anything she wanted to! In my mind I would justify it. I would tell myself that I liked him and the age gap really wasn't that bad. He liked everything about me and would often want me to stay longer than I did. He would offer me more and more, and I would lie to him and steal from him and cheat on him. One night I spent the night, and he asked me to clean up his office the next day. As I was cleaning up his office, I came across one of his checkbooks, and I stole it. That day as I was pulling out of the driveway, I knew I wouldn't be back for a long time because I was about to go on a spree with his checkbook, and that is exactly what I did. I went shopping. I wrote big checks to myself. I started taking my friends to Splash

Kingdom and other places. During this time my mother was inviting me to church all the time. The church she was inviting me to was at "The Ramada Inn." LifeBridge had rented out a big room in the building, and they would meet there for church. I would go every now and then, but I would be strung out or loaded when I walked in usually. I would also bring questionable people with me when I did come. I had this crazy stupid idea one day when I had nowhere to go…what if I used one of these hot checks for a hotel room at the Ramada Inn? Right next to the church…I stayed in a hotel room and did drugs in it and filled it with more and more stolen things. When the money and the checks ran out, I called the front desk and told them LifeBridge would be paying for a week for me because I was speaking at one of their conferences, and they believed me, so they let me stay. They started charging my mom's church for her drug-addict daughter to stay in one of those hotel rooms. LifeBridge obviously had no idea until I had racked up quite a large bill. My "good times" were about to come crashing down in the most terrible way imaginable. Little did I know, the Longview Police Department had surveillance on me; they were on to me, and they had been watching my every move. I had not only stolen checks from Otto but also from one of my childhood friends' moms, and they had pressed charges on me. I had drugs in that room, men in that room, stolen property in that room, and they were wanting to build a case on me, so when they came in, they had a lot of evidence to prosecute me on. Up until now I had only been arrested for petty theft and criminal trespassing on Walmart property. Nothing serious like *prison* serious, felony serious.

It was a hot night right in the middle of summer, and I heard a knock on my door at the Ramada Inn. I looked through the peephole and saw one of my friends staring back at me. I had no idea, but he was setting me up. He was on the other side, the good side, just pretending to be on my side…

I opened the door and let him come in, and he was acting super weird. I kept asking him if everything was okay, and he kept saying, "Look, Brittney, your whole world is about to come crashing down around you." I am like, "Yeah, I know, I have been making some terrible decisions." He scolded me for getting that hotel room under the church's name, and he scolded me for stealing those checks. He didn't mind buying the prescription pills that I had been on for opiate addiction, though. That was why he was there—his own selfish desires. He left that night, and I was all alone, and those words just kept replaying in my head...*your whole world is about to crash down around you...your whole world is about to crash down around you*...I had a sick feeling in my stomach. I had a feeling that something bad was about to happen. I could not quite put my finger on what it was...I would know in about six hours...I took one of my pills that relaxed me, lay down on my bed, dissolved that pill under my tongue, and fell asleep...

The next thing I knew, there was a knock on my hotel room door. I ignored it at first and just tried to stay in the state of sleep I was in, but the knocking grew louder and louder. Grudgingly, I got up out of the bed and looked through the peephole. There was a short, stocky lady with blond hair staring back at me. I had never seen this lady before, but I recognized something shiny pinned on her shirt; it was a badge. The Longview Police Department was there to arrest me. My heart was pounding as the knock turned into more of a banging. "LPD—open up..."

I opened the door, and they rushed me; they had a search warrant and a warrant for my arrest. They yelled, "Brittney Major, put your hands behind your back. You are under arrest..."

I had done it this time; I was in big trouble, and I knew it. I left all that stolen valuable stuff behind that day in that hotel room. LPD came in and processed it through evidence. I not only had written a bunch of checks, but I had also stolen a bunch of credit cards.

I remember something my dad told me when I started being wayward. If I ever found myself in a situation with police or investigators, I just had to tell them that I wanted a lawyer. He said, "You keep your mouth shut, and you say, 'I would like a lawyer.'"

The Gregg County Jail is so cold. I was freezing. I barely had any clothes on. They made me put on the first pair of shoes I saw by the bed, and those happened to be high heels. So here I was, getting booked into jail with high heels and pajamas on. I had no bra. I had a T-shirt and a pair of pajama pants on. Can you imagine being booked into jail with a pair of high heels and pajama pants and a shirt with no bra? You want to talk about embarrassing things. I remember the elevator ride up to the fifth floor and the walk through the sallyport was so shameful. I looked like a totally crazy person; I was thinking, *They made me wear these shoes, and I was asleep when they arrested me.* I wanted to scream that to every person giving me that sideways glance.

After I was booked in, I was taken to a room that I had never been in before. Two men come in dressed in nice clothes with some zip-lock baggies with some stolen stuff in them. I recognized the cards; I knew exactly what that stuff was. I had been going crazy with those checks and cards; *go big or go home* was my motto. What were they going to do? Kill me? I was already dead inside. I was not scared of the consequences.

"Do you recognize any of this stuff?" the first officer said. "No, sir," I spoke. "You sure about that? Because we have been watching you, Brittney. We know you are running around with these checks and cards, and you might as well admit what you have done; it would be better for you in the long run." Right then the words my father taught me came intruding into my thoughts, and I said, "I want a lawyer."

Maybe I was delusional because I seriously thought my parents were going to figure out a way to pick me up and get me out of there any minute. It never happened. The days started going by faster and faster, and I was just locked up. I became a trustee quickly. It is so weird that I could work in jail and hold down work and a job when no one paid me, but out in the world, I couldn't. I loved being a trustee in jail. The work made the days fly by, but you had more freedom. If you are a trustee, they let you have razors, more food, and more privileges, plus you get close to the guards. I liked the guards, and they liked me. They gave me a nickname; they called me "Paris" after "Paris Hilton." I felt like I was somebody in jail; even if it was negative attention, I got attention. As silly as it sounds, I liked my jail nickname of "Paris" because it made me feel pretty. I was so insecure, and I could not see myself as pretty. When I looked in the mirror, all I could see were my flaws; it was hard for me to see myself right. That is why we need spiritual eyes to see. The Lord doesn't look at the outward appearance, but He looks at the heart.

    I had choices to make. It reminds me of the garden of Eden. God says you have this beautiful garden to enjoy, but you just can't eat from this *one tree*, and what does humanity do? We eat from the tree. We must learn to live in the "free world" without accessing that tree. The lesson to be learned from Adam and Eve is He has given us this beautiful garden and these beautiful animals; we can do anything we want except for one thing! We must learn to have access to everything without entry. Right now, I can look up nasty, terrible things on my cell phone, but I must have self-control not to. There is a liquor store ten minutes from my exact location, but I must learn to drive by it without walking in it! Access to all the things without entry into them! There are vape shops, CBD, and kratom shops that I pass every single day on my way to work, but I must learn to keep going past them and not slow down the car and walk inside of them. God gives us choice. There were two trees in the garden, and He gave us free will to eat whatever tree we wanted. We must learn to use our free will with self-control and live in a world with access to all kinds of evil without participating in such evil.

As I was waiting for my court date to approach, I half-heartedly started reading my Bible again. I started going to church when they called it, and oftentimes I would see a friend of my mom. She was a volunteer at the Gregg County Jail, and she would always pray for me and tell me I was too beautiful to be in that jail. She was a very nice lady, and every time she saw me, she would pour in me and try to get me to think differently about the way I was living. I was mainly doing it because I was begging God to please let me out of that jail on probation. I just knew I was going to get probation. I would just say, "Please, Lord, I will read my Bible and everything." I prayed every night that I would get out of jail and get probation. A lot of the other girls in my tank who did worse things than me were getting probation, and this was my first time to have any felonies. I had a long list of misdemeanors, but this was my first time to commit a felony. I was also in my early twenties. Surely, they would give me another chance. I also had a baby. All these things kept me up at night. I had to get out of that place; I did not belong there. Surely the judge would see that I was not the kind of girl that goes to prison. There was no telling what would happen to me in prison. It felt like I was in a time warp, and time went by so slowly, but finally, my court date came around, and they took probation off the table very quickly. The court felt like I had a drug problem and offered me a place called SAFP. Gregg County was going to be my home for a lot longer than I wanted it to be, and even worse, I was going to prison. Real. Life. Big. Girl. Prison. I was so angry. When I got back to my tank, I picked up my Bible, opened it, and was just kind of holding it and running my hand across the pages. Then, out of nowhere, I threw it as hard as I could across the tank, and it hit the wall. I yelled at God and told Him, "Thanks a lot!" He didn't give me my way, and I was so angry at Him. I did not pick up a Bible again for a very long time. That disappointment in God was a seed that started a resentment that caused me to be bitter. If God was going to send me to prison, I was certainly not going to serve Him. I made up my mind, and I made my choice. *I am going to live for me; I am the only one who can look out for me anyway*, I would tell myself. *You can't trust anyone, Brittney*. I would repeat in my mind, *You got to take care of you*. The truth is I cannot take care of myself, I need a shepherd, I need guidance, and I need leadership. The Bible teaches the older women to teach the younger, and there is a reason for that. There is wisdom in counsel and advice and all of that. I just had to wait now—wait to go to prison. There was no way of knowing how long it would be. I was a trustee, so I worked long hours in the kitchen. I would wake up at 2:00 a.m. every morning and go to the kitchen and have breakfast ready for the *whole* jail by 5:00 a.m. I loved it. I would come back to my bunk and eat a huge breakfast and then go back to the kitchen at 10:00 a.m. and have the whole jail lunch ready by 12:00. The men cooked dinner, so we were only responsible for breakfast and lunch. I was a likable girl, and I made friends easily, so believe it or not, I made friends with all my bosses (guards who oversaw the kitchen). Mrs. Brenda is the one responsible for giving me the nickname Paris. One morning we were sitting around eating scrambled eggs, and she looked over at me and said, "Are those eggs good, Paris?"

"Why are you calling me Paris?" I spoke. "Because you remind me of Paris Hilton…" So it kind of stuck. There were a lot of jobs you could have in the kitchen. The main job was head cook, then there were pots and pans, then the "line" where the trays come, and you put food on the trays, but I *loved* spraying the trays with this giant hose that came down from the ceiling. No one liked that job because you would end up soaking wet, but I loved it. I would stand in front of the kitchen sink and spray those trays and get all the muck off and then sling them to the next girl, who would stack them and put them in the dishwasher. We would laugh and sing songs and really have fun in that kitchen. We would always ask Mrs. Brenda if we could listen to music, and she would let us, so we would sing Taylor Swift's "Love Story" and play and giggle, kind of like little girls. Like we were ourselves a little. The longer I worked in the kitchen, the closer Mrs. Brenda and I got. I found a lot of favor in her eyes; she would let me look at the men's roster to see if there were any men I knew in the jail. I would find some man and then write him a letter. She also told me that she could probably find out when I pulled chain, and she did...Mrs. Brenda was good to me. I am grateful for her. One day I reported to the kitchen early in the morning, and Mrs. Brenda looked at me and smiled. "Honey, tomorrow is the day...they are going to pick you up to go to prison..."

Chapter 6

BIG GIRL TIME-OUT

> *"Continue to remember those in prison as if you were there together with them in prison, and those who are mistreated as if you yourselves were suffering."*
>
> Hebrews 13:3 (NIV)

I pulled chain in August of 2008; Madisyn was five years old when I went to prison. When she would ask, "Where's mommy?" My parents would respond, "She is in big girl time-out." I missed her so much. I would write her name on everything. I would sit and draw her pictures and write her letters and call her as often as I could. If I couldn't do this for myself, I was going to try hard to do this for her. I was going to finish this prison sentence and straighten up my life for good. The guards called my name, and they gave me this paper suit I had to zip up in the front. It was blue, and I got a glimpse of myself in the mirror. I was so pale. I looked like a blueberry. How did I get here? How could a girl who was raised in a good home be in this blueberry suit on her way to prison? What had I become? I looked like Violet on *Willy Wonka* when she ate what she wasn't supposed to eat, and she turned into a giant blueberry.

My stomach grumbled on the way to the Ellen Halbert Unit. I was anxious. To be completely honest, I was scared. I had been in jail a few times, but I had never been to prison. This was a big girl's prison. I didn't know what to expect. Everything I saw in the movies made me think I was going to get assaulted or raped. I really was nervous. I was twenty-three years old. I wondered if there would be anyone else in there my same age. I wondered if I would make a friend. The transporter driving me there asked me, "Hey, how do you know Colby?" "He used to date one of my friends," I responded to her. "Yeah, well, he is my nephew, and I am just wondering how he got mixed up with a girl like you." *How rude*, I thought to myself, but I wasn't trying to pick a fight with the woman who was dropping me off at prison. "Nah, it's not really like that. He just used to date one of my friends a long time ago, and we hung out the night I got arrested—that's all." I couldn't help myself. "I'm sorry, but how did you know I was hanging out with your nephew?" I asked her. "The camera you had on when you booked in, part of all that stolen property found in your room—it had pictures of him and you and other people on it, and I saw it." *Wow*, I thought to myself. *When is the last time detectives let transporters go through stolen property and look at their pictures?* "Um, I need to go to the bathroom," I said, looking down at the shackles on my hands and feet. "I can pull over, but you have to be shackled until you get in the stall, and then I will take the chains off," she said. "Okay, like in front of people?" I asked. "Yeah, we will have to go to a public restroom like at a gas station or something." "Okay," I responded.

When we got to the gas station, I had to go bad enough that I didn't pay much attention to what everybody thought of me, but I am sure they were thinking I must be a Hannibal Lector who was chained at the hands and feet for a reason. It was so embarrassing. I don't ever want to feel that way again. Just total vulnerability, like, *hey, guys, here I am shackled at the ankles and wrist, no big deal—hope everyone has a good day.* We pulled up to the prison surrounded by a ton of green land and barbed wire. My transporter came around to my door and opened it and started walking me with my hands and feet chained up to the door. The first thing they made me do was strip down and take all my clothes off. How embarrassing—my face was blood red; there was no getting used to this. It was just shameful. The TDC guards searched me and cleared me and then pointed me to a shower that I had to use before they would walk me to my dorm. After I showered, they threw me some white clothes and ugly black shoes and told me to put those on and walk with my hands behind my back. I followed them to a big dorm. I kept my hands behind my back and did exactly what I was supposed to do. When I reached the dorm, a different lady said, "Here is your bed. You are thirty-eight. If we call for thirty-eight, that is you." I studied the dorm, and there was a number on every bed. Mine was thirty-eight, but it went all the way up to sixty-eight. There were sixty-seven other women I was about to live with in this dorm. *Great, I thought to myself, just great.*

The first week in prison is the hardest. It seemed like they called my number every ten minutes. The only problem was I was not used to being called a number, so other women were constantly having to remind me I was thirty-eight and I needed to report to the front. I studied everyone. I just sat and watched, and one girl that I thought was funny and it would be cool to be her friend came over to me. Her name was Jaime.

"Have you seen the warden yet?" she said. "Nope, I think I'll do that tomorrow," I said. "Okay, well, just to give you a heads up…tell him that you know how to mow and sow, you do not want to get a kitchen job, and if you don't have some kind of skill, they will put you in the kitchen, and you will hate it there."

"I don't know how to mow or sow," I said. "That's okay; they will teach you—just say it. I am in the laundry room, so maybe you will get put there with me." The next morning, I got called in by the warden of the unit. He asked me, "Do you have any skills you want to tell us about?" "Well, sir, I know how to mow and sow…" I lied. "Great, we will get you assigned to a job tomorrow," he said. *That was easy*, I thought. The next morning came, and just like clockwork, I heard them yelling, "Thirty-eight, come get your work slip." I walked over to the gate and pulled a small white piece of paper out of the guard's hand. I looked down to see what it said. I saw "front yard squad." Mowing. I was going to be mowing. Normally, this wouldn't be a problem, but I had never run a lawn mower in my life. I was kind of wishing that I did not take my new friend's advice. Laundry, I can do. Mowing, I cannot do. I had done laundry several times—mowing…never once.

The next morning, I woke up at 4 a.m. to get in line for breakfast. I ate breakfast, waited in a long line to get some laundry traded out, and then off to my first day on the front yard squad. It was still dark outside when we started. Captain Kirk, a peculiar country-looking man with a large brown mustache, yelled out, "If you are on the front yard squad, line up here!" I lined up and did as I was told. We loaded up to go to the shed where all the mowers and weed eaters were. When we arrived, all the girls started grabbing mowers, so I followed suit. I got a little confused, and I guess I was staring at one of the mowers when Captain Kirk shouted, "*Major*"—my name was Brittney Major, so he was calling me by my last name—"you ain't never ran a lawn mower in your whole life, have ya?" I said, "No, sir, I have no idea what I am doing." He came over and gave me clear instructions on how to choke it and how to crank it, and it worked like a charm. Then he pointed me to a large field and said, "Okay, get after it."

Music was such a huge part of my life. I listened to very demonic music. The lyrics were so powerful, they would sort of lift me and put my mind and my soul in a different place than Burnett, Texas. I would push that mower and just sing those lyrics, and when I would get home, I would write lyrics. I loved music so much; that was how I spent a lot of my time—singing and writing. Every day when I got the metal of the lawn mower handle gripped in my hand, I would begin to listen and sing those songs in my head, on repeat, every single day.

My parents decided not to bring Madisyn to the prison to see me, so I went a long time without seeing her precious face. That was probably the hardest part about prison. I missed Madisyn. I missed my parents. They brought her one time to see me, and it was the hardest visit I have ever had. She looked at me, and I just started crying. She was my reason. I remembered her and that I needed to get my life cleaned up for her. I had not seen her in five months, so the first time I saw her, it carried me through the rest of the time I had to do. The funny thing about jail and prison is when you feel like you just can't take it anymore, you get a visit, and you see people who love you, and all of a sudden, you feel like you can do hard things again. You leave that visitation room remembering that someone cares for you, and if you can't do it for yourself, you should do it for them. I began to think that maybe I could do this clean, sober thing. I had a love interest when I got locked up named Luke, and he would write to me and send me money every now and then when he could. The relationship between Luke and I was a weird one. I had started off dating his cousin and falling in love with him, and somehow, I ended up being with Luke. I was such a train wreck that I really didn't know what a relationship was, much less how to be in one, but he would at least act like he cared that I was in prison. The funny thing about being locked up is you find out who is there for you and who is just faking it. A lot of people fake it. It is what it is. As soon as you get locked up, they disappear...poof...gone. Sure, they tell you they will always be there, but they aren't. When I was in the county, I had sooo many people tell me they would write to me and they would be there, but every one of them fell off except for my parents and Luke. It does start to mess with your self-esteem because you start thinking maybe you aren't worth the wait, ya know? I wish I could say that prison changed me and turned me into a different person, but I can't. Prison doesn't change people; only Jesus can do that, and at the time, I was mad at Jesus. I felt if I read my Bible and prayed a little bit in the county, then I would get released. God would let me go; like a genie in a bottle, I would rub the lamp and make my request and do what the genie wanted me to do. That is how it worked, right? I was willing to do just a little tiny bit of Christianity but not the whole thing, not lay my life down. I couldn't do that.

  In prison, I read a lot of books and found a very close friend. She thought I was hilarious, and we would spend hours talking and playing Scrabble. I was the only girl in my whole tank who loved football. Every Sunday I would be all by myself in the day room watching football while all the other girls would take naps. I missed my dad, and football made me think of him. I always thought he was watching the Dallas Cowboys game with me somehow because he was at home and I was in jail, but at that moment we were watching the same thing. The Cowboys games made me feel close to my dad on Sundays, even though I was watching on a tiny screen by myself, and no one was in there with me. It was like a little piece of home in the middle of a jail cell. The same feeling came when I walked outside. Even though I was very far away from Madisyn, I would look up in the sky and think she was under the same moon as me, and that made me feel close to her and brought me comfort. I started off in the front yard squad, and I ended up being a can crusher. Being a can crusher is cool because you get to put on these really heavy-weight boots that look kind of like rain boots, and you get to just crush aluminum cans with your boots. Talk about anger management? I would get out there and go to crush those cans and take out all the anger that I felt in my heart. I liked that job, and it was way better than being in the heat. I did not get a lot of mail, but when I did, it sure did make the days better. Luke wrote to me and my mom and my brother, who was also locked up at the time. Every now and then I would get a letter from somebody in the county or some random person from my past, but most of the people forgot about me.

 Eventually, I made friends with Burnet, Texas. I started getting into a routine and doing the same things every day. I took a class that helped me a lot. Slowly but surely, I was getting my confidence back and starting to feel like myself again. It was good for me. The time went by slowly, but finally I received my slip that gave me my release date, and I was ecstatic. When you get your release date from prison, they send you down to the laundry to get your measurements so you can write to your family and tell them what size clothes you need. My measurements were crazy, so crazy. I remember telling my mom, "There is no way I wear the size they are telling me, Mom." I went into prison in a size zero, and when I told my mom what clothes to get me, I needed a size thirteen. I had grown thirteen sizes. It makes me laugh on the inside because all they feed you in jail is pork and noodles and all things bad for you. Plus you get to go to the store and get Blue Bell and Coke and more things bad for you. I was going home, well, sort of like home. I was going to a halfway house the state of Texas chose for me; that was the next step to all of this. So I was close to being home. I was so close.

Chapter 7

HALFWAY HOME BUT NEVER MADE IT

> *"It is for freedom that Christ has set us free. Stand firm, then, and do not let yourselves be burdened again by a yoke of slavery."*
>
> Galatians 5:1 (NIV)

My release date was February 17th, 2009; it was cold that day, but to be honest with you, I wouldn't have cared if it was thirty below because I was about to taste freedom for the first time in almost a year. I could not wait. My mother was so good to me. She had some cool clothes sent to the jail for me to go to the halfway house. It was like Christmas Day opening that box and seeing those clothes. Every single day for the past year, twice a day, I had to strip down naked in front of someone and let them search me. It was terrible, so being able to go in a bathroom and shut a door and put on clothes without having to strip butt naked and squat and cough felt like the greatest freedom. I wore a white Aeropostale shirt with gray snowflakes on it, a pair of jeans, and some green shoes because the writing on the white shirt was green. I had made a friend in prison; her name was Samantha, and believe it or not, we got released on the same day, and somehow, we ended up going to the same halfway house. It was so crazy because that rarely happens. The guards let us change, and when I came out of the bathroom, I looked at one of them and said, "Okay, what's next?" She told me to walk out this door right here and look for a van, "That van is going to pick you up and take you to Beaumont, Texas, and you just check in with them when you get there." I had never been to Beaumont; I was again anxious but so happy to be free. You would think that I would make better decisions and better friends, but Samantha and I were in for trouble immediately. The first thing she said to me was, "Let's get some cigarettes. I cannot wait to have a cigarette."

After all that time we did without smoking, we just both walked right back into bondage! How foolish we were! Proverbs changed my life for the better. The book of Proverbs teaches us about foolishness and wisdom, and it says that "as a dog returns to his own vomit, so a fool repeats his folly" (Proverbs 26:11, NKJV). I was that dog that day. A nice lady picked Samantha and me up, and off we went. The first stop we made at the gas station. She and I both went in and got cigarettes, and the driver let us light up right there in the van, so we chain-smoked the whole time in the back of that van. We smelled like a bowling alley by the time we reached Beaumont.

Thirty minutes after I was released from prison, I went right back into that vomit. I started puffing those cigarettes that I had been free from for so long. That turned out to be an addiction, too, just like drugs. I had to have them. The halfway house required Samantha and I to get a job. Sam had some connections there in Beaumont, so she was able to find us a job for a cleaning service called "Kings Cleaning Service." It was a great job, and I enjoyed doing it. I have always loved to clean, so it was sort of a natural thing for me to do. I had never been on public transportation in my life, but we were required to use it. No one was allowed to have a vehicle, so we rode the bus every day to work and every day back to the halfway house. One day on our bus ride back to the halfway house, I met a guy. He was a nice-looking guy with blond hair and blue eyes, and he had a lot of tattoos. He was kind of flirting with me on the bus, and I ended up running into him quite often. He was at a halfway house, too, and was also fresh out of prison. "Perfect person to get involved with..." said no one ever. The biggest rule at the halfway house was absolutely no cell phones. Having a cell phone was a big no-no. I made it up in my mind—a cell phone was exactly what I needed. I could talk to this new guy I met. I could call my old friends that I used to hang out with. I could text; I could play games. I had to have one.

We got a free phone call once a week. Mostly, I would call my parents, but when I needed something sneaky done, I would call Luke. I called Luke and was just shooting the breeze until the counselor got just far enough away that she couldn't hear me. "I need a cell phone," I whispered. Luke told me that he was about to send me a purse in the mail. He said he had a buddy who got a good deal on some designer bags and asked me which one I wanted. He said, "I got Gucci, Chanel, Coach. What kind of purse do you want?" I told him I wanted a black Chanel bag. He explained to me that the phone would be in the lining of the purse hidden when he sent it. Yes, finally, I was going to have some communication with the outside world again. I was so excited about that cell phone.

We got visits on the weekends, but Beaumont is a pretty good distance from Longview, so I was not able to get them often. I will never forget the day that I got to see Madisyn. The last time I had seen her, she had long, beautiful curly hair; it went all the way down to her hiney. I had a precious memory of her in my mind and the way she looked and how she talked. To pass time in prison, I would doodle all the time. I came up with a funky font that I created all by myself, and I would write Madisyn in that font all the time. I would daydream about my sweet little girl. She really was one of the main reasons I woke up and at least tried to work. I probably would have skipped out of the halfway house from the very beginning if it wasn't for Madisyn. I didn't love myself too much, but I loved her.

She came running to me and jumped in my arms…she said, "Mommy, I made you a cake." I immediately started crying. It had been so long since I got to hug her. That was such an amazing day. My mom bought cake and presents and all kinds of stuff.

Madisyn's hair was gone; her grandma had cut it all off. I don't know why, but that just broke my heart. It is so hard seeing your child changed and grown up and you missing so many important things. For some reason I was so happy to see her but so heartbroken at how our relationship turned out at the same time. Thank God for my parents. Thank God they stepped in her life and showed her what a marriage between a man and a woman looks like. Thank God they took her to church and lived godly lives in front of her. You see that more and more often these days, grandparents are raising their grandchildren. I commend every one of them. I pray the Lord strengthens them in their inner man and helps them to keep going and keep fighting for their bloodline! The day Madisyn left Beaumont was a very dark day in my mind. I went back to my bunk, and I got under my covers, and I just cried. I missed her. I wanted to be her mom. I didn't want to keep messing up, but someone else was controlling me and calling the shots. I wanted to do good, but there was nothing good in me. I wanted to get clean, but I was filthy. I needed someone to save me from myself...

The package finally arrived, and I got my black Chanel backpack in the mail. All the staff at the halfway house said, "Oh, girl, this bag is so nice..." I was having a heart attack on the inside because I knew that the cell phone was in there and they were obligated to search every package. They gave it one look over and just handed it to me, phone and all. I said, "Yeah, it is really nice. I like it a lot. I am going to lie down and call it a night." As soon as I went to my room, I went into the bathroom and shut the door and began to tear the lining in the bottom of the purse, and there it was: a cell phone and a charger.

Sin is fun for a season. The cell phone seemed like a great idea. I could talk to all my people again. I would talk to Luke, but I would also talk to Doug, and that turned into a romantic relationship quickly. I met up with Doug after I got off work, and he seemed so excited. He said, "Guess what?" I said, "What? Why are you smiling like that?" He said, "I got a hotel room for the weekend for you and Sam and me and my friend." I was just coming up on a weekend pass, and my plan was to go home and see Madisyn and my parents, but Doug was throwing a wrench in all of that. "I don't know. I think I am going to Longview to see my folks and my little girl." "Just come with me. You can go home next weekend; we can get some drinks if you want, drink some, and relax and hang out. Just us—come on,

Brittney." I caved. "Okay," I said, "but we have to be super careful not to get caught." "Just tell your halfway house you are going to Longview and meet me at the room. I will have the alcohol and cigarettes and everything we need," he said. So there I went. Like a lamb to the slaughter. Sam and I lied. We signed out of the halfway house as if we were going home to see our family, and we slipped right into that hotel room and got drunk and smoked and did stupid stuff the whole weekend.

I felt gross come Sunday night. I didn't even know this guy, and I was sleeping with him and risking my entire freedom for him. I was such a foolish girl. Why did I keep doing this? I remember being sick to my stomach for a week after that. I was still talking to Luke every day, and I knew he would never talk to me again if he found out about Doug, so I was just lying to everyone around me. I had turned into quite a liar. The Bible says, "You belong to your father, the devil, and you want to carry out your fathers' desires. He was a murderer from the beginning, not holding to the truth, for there is no truth in him. When he lies, he speaks his native language, he is a liar, and the father of lies" (John 8:44, NIV).

The devil had such a stronghold in my mind. He would encourage me to lie and to be unfaithful and to do things that made me ashamed. He wanted me to be in total bondage, and he wanted total control over me so eventually he could kill me. I just played right into his hand. I listened to the lies, I did what I wanted, and it always left me more broken and sicker than when I started.

Chapter 8

WHEN HAVIN' A CELL GOES WRONG

"For God is not a God of disorder but of peace—as in all the congregations of the Lord's people."

First Corinthians 14:33 (NIV)

Rules are in place for a reason. God is a God of peace. The Bible says, "For God is not a God of disorder but of peace." Typically when you follow the rules, you will live in peace. If you don't want to get a speeding ticket, you drive the speed limit. If you don't want to get in a fight, you don't start cussing people out at Walmart. Not me. I wanted the fight, I guess. Of course, it got around the halfway house that I spent the weekend at a hotel getting drunk with Samantha and two random guys. It also got around the halfway house that I lied about going on pass with my family. Again, the walls started to crash down around me. The halfway house had given my boss permission to pick me up for work in the mornings. She pulled up, and I climbed in her truck and shut the door. "Good morning, Mrs. Becca," I said. "Morning, Brit, how'd you sleep?" "Hmm, not too good. I got a lot on my mind, ya know?" "Well," she said, "I've been meaning to talk to you about something." "Oh yeah. What's that?" I said hoping she didn't catch wind of all the crazy stuff I had been doing. As far as I knew, she liked me, and I had a lot of favor in her eyes. "Brittney, you are the hardest worker on my crew. You do a great job, and you do it fast. I have been thinking about promoting you and having you lead your own team and paying you some more money, and maybe you could stay here in Beaumont and start your life over. You could get your daughter back and get you an apartment here. I feel like I can trust you, and I think it would be a good move, and I will help you in any way that I can." I was flattered. I could not believe she was saying that. "Yes, ma'am," I responded. "I think I would like that a lot. I mean, I would have to talk to my parents and everything, but I think that would be something I would like to do, and maybe it would be good for me. I need a fresh start. I think you're right. Maybe leaving Longview and all those bad influences would be the perfect thing for me to do." We cleaned a bar that day. I had a little extra pep in my step thinking of our conversation. I felt valued and excited for the future...little did I know my future was about to look a lot different than what we had talked about in that truck....

I got home late that night, a little later than usual, and when I walked in the dayroom, something felt different. Honestly, my conscience was messing with me because of the decisions I made, but life kept on, so I kept on with it. The next morning was no different than any other. I woke up around 6 a.m., I brushed my teeth, and I started getting ready for work with Mrs. Becca at Kings Cleaning Service. I was planning on having a great day, but when I walked in the dayroom, I saw some officers in there, and I was thinking to myself, *What in the world are these officers doing at the halfway house?* Right in the middle of that thought, I saw a shiny badge that said "Gregg County Sheriff's Office." I was in shock; they were there to get *me*. I was the only person in that house from Longview, Texas. The only thing that made sense to me was they were picking me up. I ran back into my room, and I emptied my pockets. I gave my cell phone and the cash I had on me to Sam, and I told her, "Here, hold this. I am about to go to jail." She was like, "No way, girl. There's no way." I said, "Yes, there is. Gregg County is in the dayroom, and I am the only one here from Gregg County." I walked back into the dayroom, and sure enough, they started walking toward me and asked if I was Brittney Major. I said, "Yeah, that's me...what exactly am I getting arrested for?" The officer looked down at a paper he was holding and looked back at me and said, "It looks like we are picking you up today for possession of a cell phone, which is considered contraband in a therapeutic community. It is also a violation of the probation you were put on out of Gregg County."

I had never heard of this charge before. It puzzled me. Just when I was thinking about turning my life around and staying in Beaumont, boom, I got punched in the face. I could understand being violated for the drinking and the lying and all the things that transpired that weekend, but I just sat in the back of that cop car thinking, *That stupid cell phone, I just had to have that cell phone. That little device got me in so much trouble, and now I am going back to prison, and I have not even made it home since the first time I went to prison.*

One small choice can change the trajectory of our lives. We must be faithful with little. Jesus says in Luke 16:10 (ESV), "One who is faithful in very little is also faithful in very much, and one who is dishonest in a very little is also dishonest in much." Jesus is teaching us that it is the little things that matter. We must learn to be faithful in the little, and then He will trust us with more. The decision to have a cell phone would keep me away from Madisyn and my family even longer than I was originally supposed to be. Cell phones are still an issue in today's culture. We stare at the iPhone more than we read our Bible. The cell phone is an idol. God taught me that I don't need a cell phone, and if I have one, I use it to preach the gospel, and I use every platform I am given to give Him more glory! I just didn't get that as a young woman, but I know that now!

I booked into Gregg County again late that afternoon. All the guards were giving me a hard time, saying, "We saved your bed for you, Brittney. Since you like it here so much, you just want to live here now? We can set you up in the back if you want us to." They put me immediately back in the trustee tank, and I just waited. I waited to see when I would go to court, I waited to see my lawyer, and I waited to see my family. I was starting to take on the identity of a criminal. This was my eighth time to be arrested, and I was beginning to spend a lot of time in Gregg County. I was getting more and more strangely comfortable in those walls. I would always work. All eight times I was in the trustee tank, and this one was no different. After a month, my lawyer came to see me. I was thinking, *Surely, they are going to let this cell phone thing go*, but they did not. They wanted to violate my probation for good and give me state jail time, and that is exactly what they did. I was gone from my family for sixteen months sitting in jail. It was miserable. Especially not being there for Madisyn. While I was sitting out that time, her grandma served me papers and basically took most of my rights. I wish I could say this time in jail really woke me up, but it did not. There would be many more times to come before my great awakening.

Chapter 9

TWIN TIME

"But where sin increased, grace increased all the more."

Romans 5:20 (NIV)

Luke and I stayed in communication while I was locked up. When I finally got out, he and I would see each other. I promised everyone I was done with the drug life. I told my parents until I was blue in the face that I would not go back. I had learned my lesson. I tried in my own strength, and we all know how that goes. Proverbs 3:5–6 (NKJV) says, "Trust in the Lord with all your heart and lean not on your own understanding." I leaned a lot on my own understanding. My parents were living in Dallas at the time, so I went to stay with them, and I got to see Madisyn on the weekends. Luke came to Dallas to see me a few times, and I would drive to Longview to see him as well. My dad and Luke didn't get along too well. I was daddy's girl, and I don't think anyone would have ever been good enough. The more I drove to Longview, the more I found myself wanting to stay. All my friends were in Longview, and my grandmother, my nana, was my dad's mom, and I loved her so much. She was a wonderful Christian lady, and she would take me in when my dad and I would fight, and he would put me out. She always had my back. She lived right in the middle of town, so I would stay with her and be close to everyone and everything. Otto had also contacted me after I got out. I was literally in prison for stealing his checkbooks, and he just wanted me to come right back over and get right back involved in his life. I was grateful for a second chance, but I thought that was strange. Otto tried to be a good friend to me, as good a friend as he could be with someone who had broken his trust time after time, and he did not care too much about the risk of me robbing him blind. Lust is a weird thing; it can really grab hold of a man. I didn't have any feelings for him, but I needed the money. Otto had even helped me get a car. Otto paid me, but Luke was who I had feelings for. Neither of them knew about the other. I was always like that, never faithful, always hiding, and cheating and lying. After prison my feelings for Luke grew stronger, and our relationship started getting more serious. Luke and I started hanging out so much that I started staying at his apartment overnight a lot. I quit seeing Otto, and I quit seeing his cousin, and I was just with him only for about six months.

I was working at Outback Steakhouse, and one night I got sick, and I called Luke and asked him to take me to the hospital. We went to the hospital, and they were running all kinds of tests. I thought that I had a stomach virus. I was throwing up and just could not shake the nausea. When the doctor came in, he introduced himself and said, "Well, we ran some tests, and it looks like…you are pregnant." "Wait, what?" I said. The doctor repeated himself and said, "Your blood work came back. You are definitely pregnant." Luke was asleep in the room, and to be honest we were both in total shock. I was so scared. My heart had been broken over Madisyn for a long time, and I promised myself I would never go through that kind of pain again. Losing her destroyed me on the inside, and it ate me up. I thought about it all the time. I thought about her all the time and how I couldn't be there for her when she needed me. It really traumatized me to lose Madisyn, and I did not ever want to be a mom again. The next morning I remember telling Luke, "I can't do this. I can't be a mom. I am no good at this. I will mess this up—I know me. I can't do this." Luke told me we didn't have to if I didn't want to; he said he would look into some other options. The other option ended up being an abortion. Even though I never thought I could have an abortion with all my Christian roots and my background, we made an appointment to Planned Parenthood in Shreveport, Louisiana, and we drove there. The morning we were to leave for Louisiana, I cried. I looked at Luke and said, "I am no good at this mom thing. I wish I was, but I am just not." He tried to encourage me by telling me that I was good with Madisyn when he saw us together and that maybe I could do it if I tried and if I wanted to. I did want to deep down, but I also wanted him to want to. I think we both probably thought the other didn't want a baby, but deep down, I think both of us would have rather had the baby.

Planned Parenthood was a strange place. I felt like I was almost in a dream state, watching my body walk in and check in. Luke came with me, and for some reason he wanted to record what they told us, so he had his phone and camera ready. The staff were nice enough, and they led me to a room where I had to sit and wait for the doctor for a consultation. The doctor came in, and an older man with glasses and salt-and-pepper gray hair explained to me the whole process and how it worked and told me that he did this every day and I would be just fine. He told me that I was in good hands. He told me the first step was confirming the pregnancy through a sonogram. I agreed, and back to the waiting room we went. While we were waiting for the sonogram, I was starting to think about what my sweet mamma and grandma would say to me right now at this moment. I could almost hear my mom saying, *Run, Brittney...*get out of that clinic. Do not sacrifice an innocent life..." I would try to shake it off and shove it down, but I did think about my mom in that waiting area. I kept seeing my mom's face, and in my mind she was saying, "Choose life, baby. You do not have to do this. Choose life and get out of this place..."

A sweet nurse called, "Brittney." I answered and said, "Yes, ma'am, that is me." "Come on back here," she said. I lay on a cold table with my blue jeans zipped all the way down and my white T-shirt up above my belly button. She squirted that jelly on my belly, and it was so cold. She took the monitor and began searching for the baby. I was watching the screen as she searched, but to me it just looked like a bunch of white clouds on a black screen. I really could not see a baby or anything that looked like a baby, but I was staring at it when all of a sudden, the nurse went, "Oh...oh my..." I looked at her in shock. I said, "What do you mean oh? What do you see?" She looked at me, and she smiled. She said, "Honey, there are *two babies* in there." I began to cry. I said, "*Two*, really, are you sure?" and she said, "Oh yes, I am sure. That is twins."

"You are pregnant with twins. See, here is one baby, and here is the other one..."

There was absolutely no way I was going to abort two innocent babies. I am not sure if I could have gone through with one, but this really changed my mind. I looked at Luke, and I said, "I am not doing this. Let's get out of here," and that was exactly what we did.

The cold jelly still all over my belly, I began to button up those jeans and high tail it to the parking lot. *Twins*, I was having twins. We got to the car, and I shut the door, so grateful I did not schedule an appointment to go through with an abortion. I didn't know how, but somehow, I was going to make this work. My mom flashed through my mind again. She would be so happy for me, she would be proud of me for choosing life, and she would help me figure out what my next steps were.

There is no easy way to say it. I was addicted to drugs when I got pregnant with the twins. Over the past seven years, I had developed an addiction to pain pills, which then turned into an addiction to the medicine they gave me to get off the pain medication, plus an addiction to anxiety pills as well. The combination of what I was taking would easily cause someone to quit breathing if they took a high enough dose, but I took just enough to numb the pain.

There is a Bible verse in Isaiah that talks about Jesus. The whole chapter is about what Jesus went through on His way to Calvary. Isaiah 53:5 (TLB), "He was wounded for our iniquities, he was BRUISED for our sins." When someone is bleeding through the skin, we can see it with our natural eye, but when someone is bleeding under the skin, we see what is called a "bruise." I believe this is a natural scientific phenomenon within the human body, but there is something deeper to be learned about bleeding and bruising.

I was bleeding when I found out I was pregnant; it was just under the skin. Jesus died for everyone who is emotionally wounded. He died for everyone who is hurting on the inside, way down deep where no one can see. The bruises on His body are proof that He cares that you are hurting under the surface and under the skin, where no one knows. He knows. I encourage you to let Him heal those bruises down deep inside of your soul. He is the *light* that needs to shine in those dark places. His glory can come in and heal you. I encourage you. Do not spend another day bleeding under the skin, holding onto things that hurt so deep inside. Call on the name of the Lord Jesus and ask Him to come and save you and help you.

"Yes, ma'am, I need to make an appointment. I just found out I am pregnant, and I need to see the doctor, and also could you put a nurse on the phone? Because I have some questions about some substances I am prescribed to take, and I don't want to hurt the babies. There are two babies. I am pregnant with twins," I said, talking quietly on the front porch of the apartment on Seventh Street. "Okay, no problem. Hold on for a few minutes, and I will get the nurse on the phone with you." I waited, and when the lady came back on the phone, I explained to her I was on prescription medicine for opiate addiction and I was taking anxiety medicine off the street.

"How long have you been on these two medications?" she asked. "I have been taking them every single day for at least six to eight months," I responded, "but I have been on drugs since I was eighteen. I was locked up for sixteen months, but that is really the only time I have been able to really be clean in the past seven years. I am twenty-five now, but I really want to do this for my babies, ma'am. I want to do what is best for them. I will do whatever you and the doctor think is best. I just don't want to quit cold turkey and hurt my babies," I explained. "All right, hun, let me place you on a brief hold and talk to the doctor, and I will be back, okay?" "Okay," I replied.

The hold time seemed like it took forever, but finally she came back and said, "Brittney, considering you have been taking these medications for so long, we are going to keep you on them. We are going to prescribe low doses throughout your pregnancy, and you will need to stop all other substances. We will monitor you and the babies. We have had other moms who have been prescribed these two medications, and they have delivered beautiful, healthy babies, so we feel like this will be the best route to go."

On the outside, it seemed like a great idea, but it was, in fact, going to keep me addicted and launch me deeper into the pit under the pretense of it "being prescribed to me," so it is okay. It is not okay to be on these substances. I don't care how long you have been addicted to pills; God wants to set you *free* from all of them. There is a freedom that God has for you that can only come by laying these addictions on the altar and letting His fire fall and burn them away. Looking back on my life, I wish I would have had this revelation sooner. I wish I wasn't given legal permission to let my flesh and evil desires take over, but I had it. I had permission to take these medications, and that is exactly what I did.

The babies were growing inside of me, and I was often wondering what they were going to be. Were they twin boys? Or twin girls? Would they look alike? As they grew, I got more and more excited about my pregnancy. I wanted these babies. I loved them. I was a mess, but maybe I could level out on these prescription pills and somehow be okay. As long as I had those pill bottles, I thought I would be. The pills were the only thing that put my mind at ease and made me feel normal. I did not feel okay at all without them. I would wake up and take my pills and be able to have normal conversations and clean up the house normally and buy things for the babies throughout the day. The pills had become my "savior"; they were "helping" me in a way no one else could.

I was five months pregnant. Luke and I were lying in bed, and my phone rang. We were watching a Lakers game, so I got up to grab it.

"Hello," I answered. It was my grandma. She said, "Brittney, I wish you would come live with me. You're pregnant, and that boy is not going to marry you and take care of you. I miss you, and we could work on some stuff around the house together, and I could help you with the babies…"

"No, Nana, I want to live with him. We are going to have babies together, so we are going to have to figure out how to be together."

My nana would always tell me, "He isn't going to buy the cow when he gets the milk for free…" and she was right. Luke and I were young; we had no idea how to raise kids or be a family. He came from a broken family, and even though I didn't, I was just as broken as him.

"I promise I will come spend time with you soon, Nana. I promise," I said as I hung up the phone.

A few days later, my Nana died. She had been so good to me all my life. She was notorious for making me the best breakfast, and she would often tell me, "If you want to have a great day, eat a good breakfast and make up your bed." She loved watching soap operas in the afternoon; she would call them her "stories." She would put me on the prayer list a lot at her small Baptist church and read her Bible a lot and ask God to help me get on track. She would always tell me she was praying for me. I have a hard time forgiving myself for stealing from her. She didn't have any money, and I stole from her when I lived with her, and that was not something I could forgive myself for very easily. It still bothers me to this day. I know God loves me and forgives me, but, man, I would do things so differently if I had another chance. I am not proud of the woman I was. It is not something I would ever wish on anyone.

She died just a few days before I found out the sex of the twins I was carrying. I was devastated. I wanted her to meet them. I wanted to spend more time with her. I wanted to just say anything to her. She would never meet these precious babies, and I would never have breakfast with her again or conversations with her again. I took it hard; it was very hard to get through that pregnancy after losing my grandmother, but somehow with the help of all the prescription drugs given to me to numb the pain, I did. I numbed it, and I pushed it way down deep into my soul, and I tried not to think about it. Sure, I cried, and I mourned the loss of my grandma, but I was becoming an expert at pushing things down and bleeding under the surface, way down deep where no one could see. I was bleeding, and truth be told, I was dying. I was getting closer and closer to death than I realized.

Her funeral was in Arkansas. All my family is from Arkansas. My homeland. I often have dreams about Arkansas. Maybe it is because my family is buried there, but God will take me back to that place in my dreams sometimes, to the place where my grandmothers, both paternal and maternal, and my father are buried.

Grief is weird, and funerals are weird, but there is such a peace when you know the person loved the Lord and is in heaven. I knew that with my grandmother, and even though I wasn't in the arms of Jesus yet, I knew that she was, and I knew that maybe if I got my life together one day, I would be with her, although I never thought that day would come...

I gave birth to Maverick and Maci on September 13th, 2010. I was thirty-eight weeks pregnant when I had them. I had a scheduled C-section because though Maci was head down and ready to go, Maverick preferred to do cartwheels right above her. He was upside down and then right side up then sideways. The doctors thought it would be best for me to just have a C-section, so that was what we did. Luke and I were young and scared but excited to meet our sweet little girl and boy. The doctor gave Luke his scrubs and told him it was time. I lay on my back as they made the incision, and tears rolled down my face. I could not believe we were here; it all happened so fast. I was about to meet the two babies that the grace of God saved from being aborted on that cold winter day at Planned Parenthood.

At 12:45 Maci came first; at 12:46, exactly one minute later, Maverick was born. They were so tiny, only weighing a little more than four and five pounds. I had never seen a baby as tiny as they were. They were perfect and absolutely beautiful. Maci had blond hair, and her skin was fair. Maverick had dark hair, and his skin was darker. I could not believe they were twins. I pictured them looking exactly alike, but they didn't. Oh, how my heart swelled with joy to look at them. It was love at first sight. All the pain of what happened with Madisyn washed away. I had been given another chance to be a mom. I felt sick for being on all those pills while I was pregnant with them. Why was I like this? Why could I not just break free from this crap? I deeply desired to be free, but the longer I took this crap, the worse it got. I was so deeply addicted now, there was no getting free. I had been working hard on these medicines every day for almost two years. Since the day I got out of prison, and now I had prescriptions, so no state or law or anything could tell me I couldn't have them. I was trapped. Have you ever felt that way before? Have you ever felt trapped? Have you ever felt like there was no way out? That is exactly where I was. Jesus says, "I am the *way*..." That means if you feel like you are trapped, there is only *one* way to get out: Jesus. Jesus is the way of escape. If only I had that revelation sooner.

Maci had low oxygen levels, so while I was all alone in my hospital room, Luke had gone home to take a shower. A nice nurse knocked on the door, and she was holding a tiny bundle. She said, "Ma'am, here is your little boy, baby B." I held Maverick for the first time, and I looked into those sweet little eyes. Maverick was and is the tiniest baby I have ever held. He only weighed four pounds. He was the most precious thing I have ever laid eyes on. As I held him, I just stared into his eyes, and he stared back, and we had a moment of bonding, just us. I felt a pit in my stomach. I loved him so much, but I was so sad I couldn't be better for him, and I couldn't clean up my life enough, just for nine little months. I felt like a piece of crap.

It was several hours into the day before I got to see Maci. I was so excited to see her. Deep down I was worried that I had caused her breathing to be bad. When they brought Maci to me, the first thing I noticed was her almond-shaped eyes. She was beautiful and tiny, just like her brother. She had the lightest blond hair, and she just looked up at me. I loved her so much. She and Maverick were the best thing that had happened in my life in a long, long time. I had been through a lot of crap to get to the place where I was now with them. I may not have been doing perfectly, but I was doing better than I normally did. I had narrowed my drug use down to prescription legal pills only, and that was really saying something for me. Shame is so cunning. I believe the reason the Bible tells us to walk by faith is that the lies of the enemy line up with what we can see. We must learn to not look at what we see in front of us but see in the spirit with eyes of faith.

The nurse came in, and she said, "Okay, Mamma, all of the tests came back on the babies, and they tested negative for all the medications you were taking. They don't have to detox. They are going to be just fine. We will keep them in the NICU for a little while, but other than that, they are perfect and healthy, and you did a great job." Tears streamed down my face; I was so happy they didn't have this poison crap in them that I had been taking. *Thank God* was the first phrase that came to mind. Thank God I didn't subject them to that crap.

A different voice traveled into my mind in that exact moment and said, "You are a piece of crap, Mom; you are never going to be able to raise these kids. You lost your first baby, and you will lose these babies too; you are never going to make it. You are never going to be clean; you might as well just kill yourself."

Unfortunately, this was the dominant voice in my head for the next three years. It was so loud and so dominant; I almost did kill myself.

I felt *empty* the first day home after leaving the hospital. Totally empty. The prescription pills were not taking the edge off the postpartum. The twins woke up every two hours like clockwork. I was not sleeping, I was on high doses of painkillers and anxiety meds, and I felt like I was losing my mind. I would just sit and stare and think, *I am so empty; I am so numb.* I felt so void of reality. Like the world was spinning and there were all kinds of things going on around me, but I was just in the middle of it, drowning, and no one could see me, and no one could save me.

Chapter 10

IT'S A SLOW FADE WHEN YOU GIVE YOURSELF AWAY

"My justice and mercy are coming soon. My salvation is on the way."

Isaiah 51:5 (NLT)

My salvation was on the way, but the devil was going to do everything in his power to stop me from getting it. The MTV Music Awards were on that night, and I stared at the screen. I had never felt this empty; usually music would hype me up, but I remember watching Eminem perform that night and feeling absolutely nothing. I was just staring right at the center of the screen feeling completely numb. Luke looked at me. "Hey, you all right?" "Yeah, I am good." Tears started streaming down. "I just feel so empty, and I don't know why. Usually these awards bring me joy, and I get excited watching them, but I have been watching them for half an hour, and I feel so sad. I feel like nothing makes me happy. Not you, the babies, TV, music, like something is wrong with me. Do you think something is wrong with me?" I asked. "Nah, probably just that postpartum stuff they talk about," he responded. "You will get through it. You'll be okay."

After my grandma died, my dad let Luke and me move into her old house. We had to pay him rent, and Luke only had one way of making a living back then, and it was selling drugs, so that was what we did. We lived in my sweet grandma's house, and we made ends meet illegally. After a few months of almost not being able to pay, I had this thought: I could call Otto. I was starting to get my body back after having the twins; that would be perfect. I just needed to lose a little more weight. I needed a little boost of energy to get me up and moving again. When opportunity knocks on the door, you open it. Luke's mom had been staying with us for a few days, helping us take care of the babies, and opportunity knocked; she had some meth, and I was going to open the door.

After the first line I did, I felt *alive* again. I felt like I could do this! I could be a mom; I had energy and felt great. I put the twins to sleep, and I took out my cell phone, and I dialed Otto up. "Um, hey...I was wondering if I could come over later. I need to make some money." "Sure," he said. "I have my massage table out, and I could use a good deep tissue massage. Be at my house at seven. Trina will let you in."

Trina was Otto's housekeeper; she was a sweet lady, and she never asked any questions. At 7:00 on the dot, she let me in, and I made my way to the back of the house so I could give Otto a massage. He had a very nice full-body massage table; it was the kind that you could put your head through so your body lay just right. I was an excellent massage therapist. I had never been to school for it, but I had strong hands, and I had a way of getting stress and knots out of people with my hands. I would usually set a timer on my phone for thirty minutes or sixty minutes and give Otto a full body massage; sometimes all I would do was give him a massage, but sometimes it would be more than that. Deception, I guess, a way I didn't have to lie about what I was doing over there. This night was different, though. Otto said he needed to talk to me. "Listen..." he started to explain, "I have a guy friend. He is a doctor here in town, and he is married, so this would have to be on the down low and totally hush-hush, but I sent him your pictures. He thinks you are a beautiful girl, and he is willing to pay you more than I can; he says $250 an hour, or if you come over and spend the night, he will pay you $500 for an overnight stay. What do you think? Do you want to meet him and try?" All my mind saw were dollar signs. As nervous as I was, "Give me his number" was all I said, and he did.

Bondage never just knocks on your front door and says, "hello, I would like to bind you and control you and take over your life"; no, it is a slow fade. One bad choice at a time, and lots of justifying those bad choices and rationalizing those bad choices and making sense of them and just desensitization of your morals.

I was nervous about calling the doctor. Up until this point, Otto was the only person I had done this with, and I had introduced Otto to my family, and I was comfortable with him. Plus how was I going to keep this from Luke? He would kill me if he knew I was involved in this kind of stuff. The devil is so crafty, he had me selling my body and selling my soul, and I didn't even realize it. When you start doing this sort of thing, you really start sinking to the bottom.

The Bible says, "Every other sin a person commits is outside the body, but the sexually immoral person sins against his own body" (1 Corinthians 6:18, ESV). God commands us to flee from sexual immorality. One of my favorite Bible stories is about a young man named Joseph. Joseph went through a lot. He was sold into slavery by his brothers, but God was with Joseph, and Joseph was a man of great character and great integrity. He was like second in command in all of Egypt, and he worked for a man named Potiphar. Potiphar's wife started getting the hots for Joseph, and she wanted to sleep with him, but when she tried, he said, "No, ma'am, I will not do what is evil in the sight of the Lord." And he ran from her. He literally ran from sexual immorality. Joseph is one of my favorite heroes in the faith because of that reason right there. He understood that would be evil in the sight of the Lord, and he wanted nothing to do with it. She told her husband that he tried to rape her, and he got thrown in prison for it, but he was never mad at God. Joseph's faith in God was so strong that he never wavered while in prison. He loved and trusted the Lord so much that he trusted Him even after being falsely accused of rape. God got Joseph out of prison, and God put him right back at the top in power over everything. He restored his life, and he restored his family to him. Joseph had a wonderful, prosperous latter part of his life because he fled from sexual immorality, and God gave him everything back.

"Yes, this is Brittney. I am looking for Dr. Smith..." I said on my cell phone later that night. "Yes, this him..." he responded. "Yeah, my name is Brittney, and Otto told me to give you a call. He said you might be able to help me out...he gave me your number earlier, and I just wanted to give you mine and see if you wanted to meet sometime this week," I said. "I would love that. I could do something tomorrow or Thursday. What works better for you? I work in my office until five, so it would have to be after five, and it would have to be out at my lake house in Gladewater. I have a beautiful lake house that I call 'Spirit World.' I am in the process of a divorce, so I can't meet at my house until she leaves, which should be any day now," he said.

Oh, thank God he isn't happily married, and I am not a total home wrecker destroying a whole marriage... I thought to myself. "I could come on Thursday at six. Would that work for you?" "It sure would. Do you have any more pictures you could send me? I really liked the ones Otto sent."

"Sure," I said. "I can get you some. I have a lot on my phone."

I was skinnier than I had ever been after I gave birth to twins. A lot of it was because of the drugs, but I was also very depressed and miserable. The more miserable I got, the skinnier I got. In my spare time, I would put on sexy clothes and take pictures of myself and send them to Otto. I would do that so it would keep him giving me money and keep me fresh in his mind. Now I was going to work my magic on the doctor as well.

Thursday came, and I was so scared. The whole way to Gladewater, I was thinking about Luke and how pissed he would be at me for doing this. He had potential to hurt me; he never had before, but I wouldn't put it past him. I would be mad if he was doing something like this. I tried to cover every lie I told perfectly. I made up a story about having to drive Otto a few hours away so he could drink at a poker game and that I would be the designated driver back as soon as he was done gambling. I had actually driven Otto to a poker game before and been the designated driver, so it wasn't a total lie in my mind. Otto was on my side, and he would back my lies; even though I had robbed him blind, he had my back. I was going to rob the doctor blind too; I was just getting started.

"Spirit World" was a good name for the lake house. I pulled up, and it was one of the most beautiful places I have ever been. Very shyly, I knocked on the door, and he opened. An older man, heavy set, short, and no hair, with glasses, opened the door. He was a warm man and seemed very gentle and sweet. Little did he know he was letting a snake in the door. We went out on the back porch and started talking about where I was from, and he poured me a glass of wine. We had a nice conversation on that porch, the wind blowing, drinking wine, but I knew what was coming; I knew what I had to do; it was never something I looked forward to. The opiates had numbed me in the sex area; I felt nothing. I never had any emotion, and I hadn't had sex with anyone for pleasure since Gabriel, my first husband. Sex, to me, was power and control, but it was also a business, especially now. I had two rich men I was sleeping with, and they had lots of nice things and lots of money. When Dr. Smith walked me through the house to show it to me, I was scoping it for all kinds of valuables. I didn't take anything the first time, but there were many more times to come.

"Okay, here is $250 cash. I also got you a present," he said. "A present?" I asked. "Yes, I got a gift for you. I would like to see you here at the lake house twice a week, so I got you a Garmin GPS and a radar detector; that way you don't get lost on your way out, and you don't get any speeding tickets if you are running late," he said. "Wow, thanks, I appreciate it," I said.

When I got home later that night, I knew Luke thought I was lying. He was wondering what the heck I needed a GPS and a radar detector for, but I explained to him it was for driving Otto around. We certainly didn't want to get pulled over while he was drinking and gambling and doing illegal stuff. As I was in the middle of my conversation with Luke, I remembered the pictures that I had sent to Dr. Smith. I had to delete those off my phone. I had to do it right now. I ran to the bathroom and pulled up that text. As fast as I pulled it up, I hit "delete." Whew, that was a close call. Luke had a habit of going through my phone, so I had to make sure I cleaned it up the best I could.

Keeping secrets keeps the soul sick. The more I saw Dr. Smith, the sicker my soul got. Luke and I were fighting more and more. Neither one of us knew how to be a parent. The bills at my grandma's house were stacking up, and my parents were taking care of Maci and Maverick more often than we did. Luke had sent me to deliver drugs once to a man, and I ended up getting into a relationship with that man. Luke found out about it, and he left me. He packed up his stuff and drove away with one of his friends, and I started seeing that guy more since he was gone and I was free to. One day after being at Dr. Smith's house, I came home, and I saw a U-Haul in the driveway. *What in the world is going on here?* I thought to myself. When I got closer, I saw my mom carrying a box in the house. *Oh my gosh, she is moving in...* I thought to myself.

My mom and dad had been living in Dallas, but since Luke left and I wasn't able to hold down a job or pay any of the bills, they moved back into my grandma's house. At this time in my life, I needed them too. I was unraveling. I was not being a good mom to Maci and Maverick. Half the time I was out running the roads, getting high with my new love interest.

The look on my dad's face said it all. My dad was a great man. I had always been daddy's little girl. He had me late in life. He was forty-two when my mom gave birth to me, so I was for real his baby. All my siblings were much older than me. My dad had a huge personality; he was so funny, and he would light up any room he walked in. He was also charming. I think the best parts of me, I got from him. He was the kind of man who was so disappointed in me when I got pregnant with Madisyn and Maci and Maverick, but then after I had them, he fell hopelessly in love with them. He and I had not been good since Gabriel, and then my losing Madisyn made it even worse. He operated in fear, and so did I, so we butted heads a lot, both scared to be vulnerable with the other. There was no way he was going to let these twins slip from his hands. He had already lost Madisyn and me, and he was not about to lose these babies. My dad had six granddaughters but only one grandson. Maverick was his only grandson, and he was crazy about him. He would hold that little boy and play with him for hours. He used to sit him on the kitchen counter and make scissors out of his middle finger and pointer finger and point them toward the counter and walk those fingers toward Maverick and say, "I'm going to get you, Maverick." His fingers would make a sort of noise that Maverick thought was so funny, and he would laugh and laugh at Papa. My parents are named Todd and Toni, so my kids call them "Mama T" and "Papa T." Every time I looked at Maverick's little finger, Papa T was wrapped around it.

"Brittney...I don't want to have to do this, but you are forcing me to do this. Now if you don't get off these drugs and quit running around on these streets, you are going to lose these babies," my dad said.

Cold-hearted, I responded, "I am not on drugs, Dad."

"You think I am stupid? You think I was born yesterday? Is that what this is? We know you are on drugs, Brittney. Hell, look how many times you have been in jail and failed drug tests. We are not stupid, and I am telling you right now you are going to have to find somewhere else to live if you don't leave these drugs alone and these men alone. We are not going to help you anymore. I can promise you that," he said.

"Fine. Don't help me. I don't want your help anyway. I am leaving, and I don't care if I ever come back or I ever see you again," I said angrily.

"Well, you go ahead, missy; get your crap and just get the hell out of here," he angrily said.

"*Fine*," I shot right back.
I got kicked out the first day my parents came back.

Chapter 11

BETRAYAL

"Cast all your anxiety on him because he cares for you."

First Peter 5:7 (NIV)

I walked in the glass door. *This place is disgusting*, I thought to myself. "Yes, how much does it cost for a week here?"

There was an old lady sitting down, looking like she had been sitting in the recliner for years. The place was dusty. The owners of the hotel were from Germany, so they spoke with a thick accent I could barely understand. The hotel was called the "Globe Inn"; it was the cheapest and most run-down place in Longview, Texas, but when you have nowhere to go, it works.

"$250 for a week," the old man snapped back at me. "Great," I responded. That was exactly how much I made seeing Dr. Smith, so at least I could have a place to stay for a week. I would figure out the rest later.

"Room fifteen, it's all the way in the back. That's where your room is, and you will have to check out on Friday if you don't pay me for another week," the old man said. "Okay," I responded. "Sounds good. I may have to get another week at the end of this one. I don't really have a place to go, so we will see what we can work out."

This was the beginning of homelessness for me. Up until this point, I always had a place to stay; even if it was at Luke's apartment or a friend's house, I had a place to lay my head, but I was determined; I did not want to count on anyone. I was going to do this all by myself. I could take care of myself. I had prescription drugs that were the best kind on the street and so easy to sell, plus I was seeing these two men who would pay me. I would have to work a lot, but I could do this. *I must do this. I must be on my own.* My thoughts were toxic. The thoughts were mainly self-pity. *Nobody loves you, Brittney. If you want things done, you are going to have to do it yourself. Your parents are evil, your parents hate you, and they aren't for you; they are just like the rest of them. They will take your babies and leave you in the dust. You don't deserve those babies anyway. You are just a piece of crap, and you might as well just stay away from everyone and make a new life for yourself,* I would think to myself often.

Most of us are hungry for control. I know I was. The reason I wanted to do things on my own was that I wanted control over my own life. If I stayed with Luke, I had to do what he wanted. If I stayed with my parents, I would have to do what they wanted me to. I wanted to do what I wanted to do.

Gabriel's mom put me on child support. There was no way I was going to pay her a dime for Madisyn. I hated her for taking Madisyn from me. I would just make this money illegally and not have to pay her anything. Little did I know there was something called "contempt of court"; if you violated a court order, and if the other party wanted to bad enough, they could put you in jail for not obeying it. Gabriel's mom put me in jail for not paying child support. The first few times, they would give me a chance and set me up to go to TWC, but I never did what they wanted me to do. I was sent to jail a few times for this child support thing.

I was seeing Madisyn less and less. I had no stability. I was making it out on the street but barely. My parents didn't want me around either.

My parents were in a bit of a dilemma; they were living at my grandma's house in Longview, but they were working a lot in Dallas. My dad had a trailer on the back of his truck, and he would pick up vehicles and transport them to different places. The main pick-up place was Dallas, Texas; there are two pretty good-sized auctions in Dallas, so that was sort of a headquarters for him and my mother. The drive from Longview to Dallas every day with two small babies was tough on them. They ended up finding a place in Dallas and left my grandma's house for a short time. Obviously, I came back to my grandmother's house and immediately started my crazy shenanigans.

I was familiar with the family court system. I had been in and out of it with Madisyn and Gabriel's mom; it felt like she was taking me to court every other week. Luke and I were no longer together, and I was with my new love interest, Wes, when we got a knock on the door. I opened the door reluctantly, considering I did not know the person who was knocking.

"Hi, how can I help you?" I asked. "Hello, my name is Linda, and I work for Child Protective Services. I am here to speak with a Brittney Major," she replied. I could not believe this. Someone called CPS on me. I felt so betrayed. Who would do something like that? My mind began to race… "Uhhh, yes, that's me. Can you tell me what is going on?" I managed to get out of my mouth somehow amid the racing thought. "We had a phone call come into our office with some allegations against you, and we need to go over these allegations and do an investigation to make sure the children in this case are safe," she proceeded to tell me. "You mind if I come in for a second?" she asked.

"Ma'am, I can assure you that my children are safe. They are with my parents in Dallas; my parents help me take care of them," I told her. Maverick and Maci were little, tiny babies at this time. I was certain where they were always.

"Brittney, these allegations are that you have a paramour that you are seeing on the side and that you do drugs with this man and you are involved in some criminal activity. Would you be willing to take a drug test for us?" she asked. I was so angry, my face began to turn red. Who would call CPS and tell them that? At that moment, all I wanted was revenge. I wanted to know who called them, and that was it, and oh, I would get this person back, whoever they were. I began to question all the people I ran with. "Sure, I will do whatever I need to do," I told her.

I was ruffling through the paperwork in my hand as she pulled out of the driveway. *Paramour? What is a paramour?* I wondered. I pulled out my phone and googled it; the response said, "A secret or illicit lover." Someone called CPS and accused me of being on drugs and having a secret lover. It was all true, of course, but how dare someone call me crap like this? Who would tell on me this and try to take my kids away?

We are supposed to cast our anxiety on Jesus. Man will always let us down, but not Jesus. Jesus is supposed to be a fortress for us, a place where we can run and hide and seek shelter from the storms of life. He is supposed to be the first person we go to in times of trouble. For some reason, I had this backward. I would seek man first, and then, very last resort, I would ask Jesus. He wasn't the Lord of my life; He was my last resort.

I sought refuge in Luke. He was Maverick and Maci's dad, so it made the most sense for me to call him and tell him what some awful person did to me, how they said these terrible things about me. He would understand.

I met up with him at a gas station, and he got in the car with me. I was crying, and I said, "Someone called CPS on me concerning the twins. They said I was a terrible mother, and I was on drugs, and I had a secret lover and all kinds of stuff." Luke told me he was sorry that this had happened, but he also warned me that maybe I should clean up my life a bit, try to hold a job down, and stop running the roads. I shrugged him off and went home.

The CPS case on top of what was going on with Madisyn was eating my lunch. I started going to the bars and drinking the pain away. I never could find the answer in that bottle. Miraculously, I passed my drug test for CPS. I failed my drug test for opiates and benzodiazepine, but I had prescriptions for both of those, so it was a pass according to the state of Texas. I gave temporary guardianship to my mom and dad because I had a lot of work I was supposed to do, and I knew in my heart I probably wouldn't finish it. I was supposed to go to parenting classes and take random UAs. During the midst of all this stuff going on, I turned to Luke again. He came over, and I demanded that he call my case worker and tell her what kind of person I was. I demanded that he help me get our kids back from my parents. I wanted Maverick and Maci without having to have supervision. I missed them. I wanted to be a mom to them. "I told you I was no good at this." I cried. "Just call CPS—ask for Linda. Please help me, Luke."

Luke called CPS and asked for my case worker as I looked at him with tears streaming down my face. He was holding the phone in his right hand, and I tapped his shoulder. "Put it on speaker. I want to hear what she says," I said. Luke did as I asked, and he put the phone on speaker. "Yes, Mrs. Linda, this is Luke, and I was just wanting to talk to you about the case against Brittney. She is my kids' mom, Maverick and Maci, and I was just going to see how much longer this case was going to be open against her and what I could do to help her. She is pretty upset and stressed out over this, and she wants our kids back. She hasn't seen Maverick and Maci in a long time because of all of this. I am just trying to help her."

I will never, as long as I live, forget the words that came through that speakerphone. "Luke, you were the one who called CPS and reported all of this, and now you are calling requesting for us to give Brittney back her kids?" Linda said, sounding puzzled. *Busted*—it was Luke. Luke called CPS on me. He hung up the phone before she could say another word. I saw red. I started swinging on Luke with all my might, punching him as hard as I could. *"How could you?"* I screamed. "How could you do this to me, Luke?" He just said, "I'm sorry. I'm sorry. I was just trying to get you off these streets." The Bible says that nothing done in the dark stays hidden; if you belong to Jesus, He has a way of bringing everything out into the light and exposing everything. I was shocked. I drove erratically all the way home.

Betrayal is demonic. Judas betrayed Jesus, and right before he did, the Bible says that "Satan entered him." I was certainly no Jesus, and now

I have forgiven Luke and moved past all of this, but at the time, it felt like total betrayal. I would get even with Luke. I would get him back.

Chapter 12

HIGHWAY TO HELL

All honor to God, the God and Father of our Lord Jesus Christ; for it is his boundless mercy that has given us the privilege of being born again so that we are now members of God's own family. Now we live in the hope of eternal life because Christ rose again from the dead. And God has reserved for his children the priceless gift of eternal life; it is kept in heaven for you, pure and undefiled, beyond the reach of change and decay. And God, in his mighty power, will make sure that you get there safely to receive it because you are trusting him. It will be yours on that coming last day for all to see. So be truly glad! There is wonderful joy ahead, even though the going is rough for a while down here.

First Peter 1:3–6 (TLB)

There is a quote that says, "The road to hell is paved with good intentions," but in my life the road to hell was paved with offenses. Isn't that true for most of us? We have a hard time getting over the injustices that have been done against us. I am here to tell you *today* is the day to let go of all of that. The Lord may be bringing a person to your mind right now that you need to forgive. Forgive that person right now. Just say out loud, "I renounce unforgiveness. I renounce bitterness. I renounce offense." Come out of agreement with it. If you do not uproot that unforgiveness in your heart, you will always stay in some kind of sick cycle. You may do good for a little while, but eventually you will go back because it is a *heart* issue, and you need a *heart* change.

By the time Maverick and Maci were one year old, I had been arrested twelve times. Gregg County was my place. I knew every judge; I knew every criminal lawyer; I knew every deputy; that was just me, my identity, and who I was. The recent events with Luke, plus the fights I had been having with my parents, were the perfect storm of events that forced me to rely on myself more than ever.

After my grandma passed away, she left an old school Mercedes behind that my dad let me drive. That car would take me to a lot of dangerous places with dangerous people doing dangerous things. One night that car drove me to a hotel room to meet up with a friend. That night I met a man who would take me down a deep, dark rabbit hole that only the grace of God and the blood of Jesus could rescue me from.

I was still sleeping with Otto and the doctor for money. I had just gotten some cash, and I was wanting to get high. I was on prescription pills, but that was boring, and I was wanting to try harder stuff. I called a friend. "Meet me at that hotel across from the American Dream over Highway 80 and Eastman…" she said through the phone. "All right, see you in a few minutes," I said. I pulled in wearing a navy blue shirt that said Bud Light across the front of it and ripped short blue jean shorts. I got out and knocked on the door. She opened the door. "What's up, pussycat? Come on in…" This girl went by the name "girl Mississippi"; there were two Mississippis on the streets during this time; one was "girl" Mississippi, and the other was "boy" Mississippi. Girl Mississippi was a beautiful girl. She was tall and skinny and had dark brown hair and dark brown eyes; her bangs hung over her forehead, and she dressed nicely. She would always have an extra accessory or two that made her look rich, like a scarf or a scarf wrapped around her head and tied in a bow or jewelry. People would never assume what we were really doing in that hotel room. Girl Mississippi always called her other female friends "pussycat."

I scoped out the room. It was myself, girl Mississippi, and two men whom I didn't know. She introduced me. "Pussycat, this is Skyler, and this is Jim…" "Hi, I'm Brittney, nice to meet you…" When I shook Skyler's hand, I could feel a connection between us. I could also tell that Jim and girl Mississippi had a thing for each other, so I stayed closer to Skyler as the night went on. I had only shot dope a few times before this, and it was not something I was super familiar with doing, but that is how all three of these people did their dope, so that night Skyler said to me, "I can hit you if you want..." I said, "Yeah, that's cool..." and he stuck the needle in my vein and shot the drugs in...the room started feeling weird, my body started feeling weird, and that was the beginning of the end for me. I had made it to the bottom of society, the lowest of the low. I did this, and I made this choice, and for whatever reason, after that night, I went so far and so hard for the devil.

Skyler wrote lyrics and liked to rap, so in the hotel he was rapping and rhyming and putting lyrics together, and I noticed he said, "Yeah, they call me Skyler...Jesus Christ, the junkie..." Obviously I had Christian roots, and that stood out to me, and in a sick way, I thought, *Maybe Skyler can help me; maybe he can save me; maybe* he *is exactly what I have been waiting for...* He looked at me, and I looked at him, and something supernatural and magical happened. We fell in love. The only problem is it was a sick, twisted love formed on witchcraft and Satan, and it would take me down the most terrible and dark road I have ever walked down...but with him, hand in hand, for some reason I wasn't scared. I felt like he knew the darkness, like he was born in it, like he could lead me; he could save me, so I gave him my hand that night. I let him in; I let him have me. I was given a nickname that night, "Major." My last name was Major, so it made perfect sense.

I was in a trance staring at Skyler. I knew him. I felt it in my soul. He looked so familiar. Where did I know him from? Sometimes drugs can give you a false sense of deja vu, but this was different. *I know him*, I thought to myself... Finally it hit me. "Skyler...have you ever gone to church before?" I tried to get the words in between him rapping... "Church? Haha, baby girl, I am not much of a church person." He laughed as he responded. "Yeah, but, like, did you ever go to church a long time ago? I just feel like I know you. Like I have seen you before at church a long time ago...do you have a sister named Leah?" I said. "Yeah, I do have a sister named Leah," he said, shocked. "That is where I know you! I know you from Cornerstone; you used to go there with your mom and your grandma and your sisters...I *knew* it," I said, so happy that the mystery of it all was solved. "Yeah, I did. That is where you know me from, so I guess we could tell people we met in church, huh?" "Yeah, we can." We laughed about that, but that is exactly what we did.

Cornerstone Church was the church I grew up in. It was a Spirit-filled church and the church that my mamma "*drug*" me to as a child. It was also the church that my mother was on the praise team at. I had deep roots in that church. Cornerstone taught me about being unashamed of the gospel and the difference between religious rituals and real-life Christianity. Pastor Tom McDaniels and his wife, Charlotte, were the youth pastors of that church, and Pastor Tom baptized me and married Mitch and me. Jimmy Lockhart and Tim Anderson are powerful, wonderful people who came out of Cornerstone, and with Skyler's mom and his grandmother, they had Sunday school and Bible study and all the things that helped sharpen iron and make disciples. Cornerstone was an amazing church, and I could not believe Skyler had been there before. It felt so right, so connected on a deeper level than just a hookup.

Skyler and I were inseparable after that night. We went everywhere together. He opened my eyes to a world I didn't know existed. The world that he lived in was based on hustle. You had to go get it, you had to make money, and you had to support yourself. He was a master thief. It was like he had an invisible cloak on when he would walk into a place to steal. He never got caught, which was weird to me because I always got caught. I fit in well with most of his friends. I was willing to hustle, and being with him was giving me more of an appetite for drugs. He took me to his house and reintroduced me to his mom and to Leah, and I got to catch up with them. I thought this was the perfect relationship and perfect man for me until the demonic started happening, and very, very, very weird, unexplainable things started to happen.

Chapter 13

DEMONS

For we are not fighting against people made of flesh and blood, but against persons without bodies—the evil rulers of the unseen world, those mighty satanic beings and great evil princes of darkness who rule this world; and against huge numbers of wicked spirits in the spirit world.

Ephesians 6:12 (TLB)

It was not long before demonic activity started showing up in my life after Skyler and I started living together. By living together, I do not mean we had our own place. We laid our heads wherever we could, mostly at his friends' houses that may have let us use a spare bedroom or a couch. Sometimes we would use the money that I made sleeping with the doctor to live in hotels. He had strange friends. The first red flag was that he and his friends liked to hang out at graveyards. That was a weekend thing that they would do, and after he and I started living together, I would go with them. They loved graveyards, and they loved Halloween. Halloween was the biggest holiday of the year for them, bigger than Christmas or birthdays or anything. These are occultic practices. You may be saying, "Oh, Brittney, Halloween is innocent; it doesn't mean I am a devil worshiper." I encourage you to keep reading this book. Halloween is an important night for pagans as well as witches and warlocks. Halloween is a holiday they use to do dark practices, such as speaking to the dead, using Ouija boards, and visiting graveyards. If you are a Christian and you have no conviction about celebrating Halloween, that is between you and the Lord. This is not a hill I want to die on; however, this is my story and my experience with Halloween. I have seen the dark side of it. I have practiced it. I never flat-out said I worshiped the devil, but my actions showed it. The Bible says, "Don't be teamed with those who do not love the Lord, for what do the people of God have in common with the people of sin? How can light live with darkness?" (2 Corinthians 6:14, TLB). Please, if you feel like you have opened the door to the devil through some of these practices, let us renounce them now. Let's say out loud, "God, I renounce witchcraft. I renounce occult practices. I renounce any doors I have opened through these practices, and I close the door in the spirit to every spirit that may have come in through one of these practices..."

It was fall, and Skyler and I had been together for a few months. We were counting down the days to Halloween so we could go to graveyards and haunted houses and spend that holiday doing drugs and drinking and just living for the devil. We did not say that we worshiped Satan, but we did. We did through our actions, and we did through the music we listened to. We listened to music from artists who did proclaim satanism and were not ashamed of it. I was fascinated with some of the darkest music. I had been fascinated by it for a long time. It was some of the same music that I would listen to as I pushed that lawn mower when I was a young woman in prison.

The strangest occurrence I think ever happened to me was a night out with Skyler after we first met. I have tried to explain it over the years, but it was a strange, unexplainable thing, but I will do my best.

It was me and a few of Skyler's friends in a car this specific night. "Can you turn the heat on? I am cold..." I said to Skyler. We were out in the woods in a vehicle, supposedly waiting on someone to bring us some drugs. There was one particular friend of Skyler's whom I did not like that much and definitely didn't trust that much, and he was sitting in the front seat, another friend was driving, and Skyler and I were in the back. They turned on the heat...I remember having been up on drugs for days and just being so weighed down and tired but trying to keep my eyes open because more drugs were on the way, so I needed to stay awake just long enough to get those in my system.

The last memory I have is looking at the friend I don't trust and then looking at Skyler...then *black nothingness*...

I wake up in a strange house; my hands are numb and burning, and I am lying on a bed I have never seen before. My body feels like I got hit by a Mack truck. I begin to open my eyes and talk to myself in my head... *Where am I? How did I get here? What happened to me?* The emotions were so overwhelming because I had no memory of what I was doing there and how I got there, and my hands were hurting so bad that I just began to cry and cry. I managed to get myself to the corner of the bed and sit up on the side of the bed, and I was in total shock. I had never seen this house before, and why were my hands on fire? Why did my wrist ache and my hands hurt? A girl walks in. She is a very pretty girl with reddish brown hair. "You all right?" she asked. "No, I am not all right," I responded. "My hands and wrists are on fire, and I can't remember anything," I said. "Yeah, apparently you have been passed out for a few weeks, and a few people have been having to carry you everywhere, but you will be okay. Your memory will start to come back. My name is Olivia. Do you remember Skyler?" she asked. "*No*, I don't remember anything, and I really want to go home. Can you please just take me home to my parents' house, please?" I cried. Right then, Skyler walked in the room and sat by me, only I had temporary amnesia, and I had absolutely no idea who he was. He sat on the bed next to me and said, "Do you remember who I am?" "*No*," I exclaimed again, "I want to go home to my parents' house right now..." I said. Skyler put his hand on my shoulder and explained to me that he was my boyfriend and that I had been out for a while but that I was still breathing and that some of the drugs we had done that night when I passed out could have affected my memory. "But don't worry. It will all come back," he said. "I love you, and I am your boyfriend, and I will keep you safe."

The only part of this whole "did too many drugs and it affected my memory" story that did not make sense was the excruciating pain in my hands and wrist. So I asked Skyler, who looked like a total stranger. I did not remember him *at all*. "Why do my wrist and my hands hurt? What happened to me?" He looked me dead in the face and said, "I don't know."

The whole thing was supernatural and very weird. I had never experienced amnesia before. I could remember who my parents were, but I had no idea who Skyler was or any of the people in the house I woke up in. My hands and my wrist felt like they had been tied, and I couldn't shake the thought that I might have been taken advantage of in those few weeks that I was apparently "sleeping." To this day I believe I was drugged by those men in that car that night. The Lord has spared my life for me to even be writing to you in this book right now. The devil was behind the curtain of that whole situation. He was trying to kill me through drugs and abuse and violent, hateful people. He wanted me to die. That is honestly how serious it is. After about two days, I got used to the fact that Skyler was my boyfriend again, but I had to relearn our entire relationship. I could not remember too many of the things we had done together. He would sort of train me; he would take me somewhere and say, "I have brought you here before you lost your memory, and we did this, or we did that." It was so demonic. I did not know that then, but I see now how the devil was brainwashing me through the control of this man. We would crash on his friends' couches mainly, and then I would work for Otto and the doctor to make money for us to get a hotel for a few days. He opened a world of shooting dope to me that I had never known before, and that was the focus of most of our relationship. The only problem with that was we were always having these supernatural occurrences happening, and having a Christian background, I knew deep, deep down in my heart that I was playing around in the devil's kingdom without the blood of Jesus to protect me, and that was a scary place to be as someone who had known the Lord before.

There were two other Brittanys that we hung out with, so I went by "Major." All three of us were pretty girls, just trapped in a lifestyle from trauma and abuse that we couldn't break free from. We had been living at the Globe Inn for over a month, and we were having a sort of party, and one of the Brittanys was there in the room. She had been sort of dating a guy fresh out of prison, and he was there, as well as a few more people. We had been shooting dope together and listening to music and were just in total debauchery that night. I remember having this feeling that I just needed to separate myself from them and get away for a little while. One of them, who went by "Roach," had a gun, and I just remember him looking at me while holding that gun in a violent nature, and it just made me feel totally uneasy.

Roach was fresh out of prison. He was a thug; he would always weasel his way into these pretty girls' hearts and homes if they had one. He would take their money, he would take their car, and he would take as much as he could from these girls. He was very crazy and very controlling. At one point he was married to a girl and had convinced his wife that he wanted them to have a girlfriend in their marriage, and they all three lived together at his wife's parents' house. I hated going over there because there was always tension between the wife and the girlfriend. It made me feel uncomfortable, but he was so controlling, and he would brainwash them both. He would do it right in front of us, too, so we all knew who was running the home. Deep down, it disgusted me. I wanted to tell the wife and the girlfriend to *run* from this guy. I just knew he was dangerous. He was a loose cannon, and he was going to hurt someone. Sometimes I would lock eyes with him, and I would see murder in his eyes. His eyes were black, a perfect match for his heart. I didn't tell Skyler this, but I was pretty much out when Roach came around. I would look for any excuse to leave. He made me feel very uneasy. I just knew in my heart that something bad was going to happen with Roach. He talked like he would murder people, and a part of me thought he really would, so I wanted to get out of the room. I was having fun the whole night until Roach showed up.

I had a friend named CJ who came and picked me up, and I just rode around with him for a little while, and we smoked dope and got high.

In the darkest part of the night, probably between 3–4 a.m., my phone started blowing up. First Skyler, then Roach. I called Skyler back since he was my boyfriend. He and I had been fighting really badly that night, and that was part of the reason I left with CJ, and he was mad that I even did that. "Hey, you called?" I asked. "You have to come back to the room right now. They are going to take me to jail if you don't. The room is in your name, and the cops are on their way, and you have to come back *now*..." He was stuttering and talking so fast. "What happened, Skyler? Why are the cops on the way?" I asked. "Brittany got shot...Roach shot her...it was an accident; he didn't mean to, but there is blood everywhere, and the room is in your name, and the cops want to talk to you..." He kept on and on... "Skyler, is Brittany dead?" My heart sank... "No, she is in the hospital. He shot her in the leg; I think she is going to be okay..." he said. I looked at CJ. "I gotta go back to the room," I said.

I got back to the room, and there were three dudes there versus Brittany, the one girl. I felt so bad for leaving her there with them. The ambulance took her away, and Roach held to his story that it was a total accident and that the gun just went off. He didn't go to jail. One thing I know for sure: Brittany had a bullet with her name on it, and she could have and maybe even should have died. Roach shot her on purpose; it was no accident. That jerk finally did it; he hurt a woman. I remember he had a crush on Brittany, and just a few weeks before, she had rejected him because of his weird wife/girlfriend situation. This day really woke me up and showed me that I was involved with dangerous people. It wasn't so much that the people were dangerous; it was that demons were controlling them, and I wasn't much better. Demons were controlling me too. Who could set us free from this?

There is only one: Jesus. There is a reason the Bible says that Jesus is *the way*. There is only one way, and Jesus is it. Jesus is the only God who died for you. Buddha did not die for you; Muhammed did not die for you. Allah did not die for you. There is one, and His name is *Jesus*. True freedom is only found in Him. Philippians 2:9–11 (NIV) says:

> *Therefore God exalted him to the highest place and gave him the name that is above every name, that at the name of Jesus every knee should bow, in heaven and on earth and under the earth, and every tongue acknowledge that Jesus Christ is Lord, to the glory of God the Father.*

We moved out of the Globe Inn and into the Sunset Inn. The Globe Inn was on Highway 80, so it was a little rougher area, but the Sunset was over by Gilmer Road. Maybe if we went there, we wouldn't have any run-ins with the police. Unfortunately, we would have another one, with a gun, and with somebody being shot at, only this time…it was *me*.

Work, work, work, hustle, hustle, hustle… My life was so exhausting. I would go get money, go get drugs, stay up days and weeks at a time, sleep for days and weeks at a time, and move from hotel to hotel. My life was a totally exhausting crap devil show. I was so exhausted that day, but Skyler wanted to get some dope and have some people over, so that is what we did. Girl Mississippi knocked on the door. I cracked it open and looked through the crack. "Hey, pussycat…" She smiled. She walked in and said she needed to talk to me in the bathroom. She and I went in the bathroom together, and she told me she got some "good stuff" and it was "fire"; she loaded a couple of needles up, and she and I got high right there in the bathroom. We started getting all dolled up in the bathroom with makeup and clothes trying to look cute. She looked at me and said, "Major, I have a gun, and it is loaded, so don't touch it." She showed it to me, and it looked like a revolver-type gun. We came out of the bathroom, and Skyler and the boys were playing music and rapping, and we were all just hanging out having a good time.

It all happened so fast, but from what I remember, Skyler and I were talking and were standing in pretty close proximity to each other when girl Mississippi pointed that revolver right at me. There was not much I could do. The gun was pointed right at me, and then, as if it happened in slow motion, she pulled the trigger, and the gun went off. It was the loudest noise I think I have ever heard. There was a high pitch that echoed through my whole head, and even though there was movement and words in the room, I could hear nothing. I ducked, and my ears were just ringing and ringing, and I could smell the gunpowder in the air. I could even taste the smoke from inhaling the gunpowder. Skyler tackled girl Mississippi and started cussing her out. He was like, "You just tried to kill my girlfriend! Why would you do that?" Girl Mississippi just started crying, saying, "Skyler, I swear I did not mean to do that. It was a total accident. I would not do that to Major—you know me..."

That night the hours went by very, very slowly. I sat on the bed thinking that I had almost died. The bullet was so close to hitting my head. It barely missed my head. That bullet had my name on it, but why? My paranoia from the meth started to kick in. Did I owe someone money? Did I sleep with someone that I wasn't supposed to? Did Mississippi secretly hate me and want me dead? Why did I almost die? Who was out to get me?

I started losing it. I was obsessed with thoughts of people trying to kill me and people having evil motives against me. I had PTSD from being drugged and possibly harmed, Brittany being shot, and then me being shot at. I can tie all three of these things that happened to demons; the Bible says in John 10:10 (TLB), "The thief's purpose is to steal, kill and destroy. My purpose is to give life in all its fullness."

The devil and his demons were literally trying to kill me, they were trying to destroy me, and they were trying to take my life, and the most beautiful part is Jesus was standing at the door of my heart, and He was knocking, and He was trying to give me life and purpose.

Strange, unexpected, and unexplainable things were happening on a regular basis. The real world seemed stranger than intense psychological thriller movies those days. The world was a scary place for me, and I could not trust anyone around me, and I could not trust myself. The deeper I got, the worse my self-esteem got, and I started believing lies that maybe this kind of life was just what I deserved. Maybe I was just destined to be some sort of roach that crawls around at the bottom of society, a homeless drug addict who every now and then thinks she finds love and friendship only to lose it again. There were many things I did in those days that I am not proud of, but looking back, I think it's as if I were a different girl. I can talk about her, the old me, because that is, in fact, not me. That is why the Bible tells us we must be born again. A new person must be born. I have enjoyed the years of being born again so much. I have enjoyed getting to know the new and different me. The things I love, the food, the colors, the animals, and babies. Before I got saved, I had no love in my heart—just couldn't love myself or anyone else. After I got saved, I fell in love with everything. I loved butterflies and trees and babies and puppy dogs and colors. It was like I was looking at life for the first time with a brand-new set of eyeballs, and it liberated me. I started discovering music genres that I liked and food that I liked. I was so codependent that I just did whatever everyone else was doing. I listened to what they listened to, and I liked what they liked, but after coming to Christ, I yoked up with Him and began to love like Jesus, and it made life actually worth living… Maybe that is you. You have been codependent for so long, you don't even know who you are anymore. I pray this prayer over you. "Lord Jesus, I thank You that You make me a new and different person when I come to You. Lord, help me to become exactly who You want me to be. Lead me into a new way of life where I am solely dependent upon You and Your plan for me. Show me how to depend on You and You alone. Show me how to forsake all others and lean into You and invite You into every area of my life. Jesus, teach me that I am never ever alone. You are always with me."

I work at a car dealership now, and I remember one day being in a meeting with some very prominent and rich businessmen and women. As I was sitting in this meeting, the Holy Spirit said to me, "Brittney, who is the richest person in this room?" I played along, and I said, "Lord, probably the owner of this fancy car dealership or maybe that guy who drives the Corvette who is a finance manager." The Holy Spirit said, "No, the richest person in this room is the person who knows Me and is in a relationship with Me."

"Wow." My eyes filled with tears. "I am rich because I know You, God." What a profound lesson I learned in the conference room that day.

Chapter 14

ANGELS

"For the angel of the Lord guards and rescues all who reverence him."

Psalm 34:7 (TLB)

I am so grateful for God our Father and our Lord Jesus Christ. He sends angels to rescue us from all of our troubles. All we have to do is call upon the name of the Lord. There is no place too dark for His presence. I have seen a lot of testimonies where people said something so simple as, "Jesus help me..." and they woke up and weren't depressed anymore, or maybe they weren't as anxious, and they felt as if they had a sound mind. The gospel is simple. Faith in Christ is simple. It is truly living for the devil that makes life hard.

In Matthew, Jesus was led into the wilderness to be tempted by the devil. He had been fasting, and He was weak, and the Bible says that the Lord sent angels to Him to strengthen Him. In verse 11 it says, "Then Satan went away, and angels came and cared for Jesus" (Matthew 4:11, TLB).

I often think about this picture. Jesus being weak and tired from the human part of himself. He was probably lying with His head resting, and the angels were ministering to Him and strengthening Him, feeding Him bread of heaven, praying for Him, possibly praising Him, and reminding him of His assignment from heaven. We also see angels in 1 Kings come and minister to Elijah in the same way. In this story, Jezebel had just threatened Elijah because he had killed her prophets, and the Lord had showed Himself mighty through Elijah, but Elijah believed that Jezebel was going to kill him, so he ran. He was all alone when the angel touched him and told him to get up and eat. He looked around and saw some bread baking on hot stones, and the angel told him again to get up and eat more because he had a long journey ahead of him. The angel fed him bread of heaven and encouraged him to *get up* and get back at it. I believe that when we are weary and we feel like dying, the Lord sends angels to feed our spirits with bread from heaven. The angels minister to us; the angels encourage us and tell us to keep going, to not look back, to run our race, and to keep going. Don't *you* dare give up. I pray right now that you feel the angels of the Lord ministering to you right now as you read this. I pray the angels whisper to your soul, "It's time to *get back up*." It is time to quit running from Jezebel and the threats of the enemy; it is time to face your enemy and watch the God of heaven's armies defeat your enemies before your very eyes. There are angels who are fighting for *you*, ministering to *you*, and strengthening *you*, just like they did Jesus and Elijah.

Angels would always show up in my life right on time and no matter what. The angels that I speak of in the natural are called "Longview Police Department." When I was in dangerous situations, out of my mind, they would show up. They would usually show up because I was breaking the law, but they would always put those handcuffs on me and tote me off to jail, and in retrospect, it probably saved my life on more than one occasion.

The year 2012 was very hard on me. I was in jail more than I was free. I had to sit in jail for six months for child support that I owed on Madisyn. You would think that would have set me up to go in the right direction, but I was bad on the needle. Once I started using methamphetamine intravenously, I started trying it with heroin as well and ended up getting addicted to heroin. There weren't many dealers in the Longview area whom I knew, so it seemed like we were with the same sketchy people all the time.

Skyler and I were quite the team. I introduced him to my parents, and they warned me that I needed to break up with him and take care of my kids. I never listened; I spiraled out of control. The more my mom prayed, the worse off I got. The Bible tells us, "Do not grieve the Holy Spirit" (Ephesians 4:30, NIV). I was grieving the Holy Spirit as well as everyone who cared about me. I would come home to visit and have track marks all over my arms and hands. I was bruised all over my body from shooting for days, and my mother would just tell me that she was praying for me. I felt too far gone, like I had crossed a spiritual line where the people go when God doesn't want them anymore. You need to know that nothing can separate you from the love of God. You are never too far away from Him. As a matter of fact, if you believe the Bible like I do, you will understand this truth: He is with you. He never leaves you or forsakes you. You are not abandoned, you are not rejected, and you are not destroyed. If you feel that way, you are just God's type. He loves chasing rebels down; He loves bringing them out and setting them free.

As I mentioned before, Skyler was a mastermind thief, and I was not. We would go into places, and he would steal us food to eat because, most of the time, we didn't have money for food. He would always tell me not to do it because I was terrible at it, and I would always get caught. One night, we went to the Shell station so he could steal some food, and I was so out of my mind that I was in the store just throwing things in my bag. The police showed up, and I went to jail for stealing and being intoxicated in public.

I stayed in jail just long enough to sober me up. When I was released, I remember I was hearing voices. I sat in my car and thought maybe I could channel these voices and ask them where to go. I did not know where Skyler was, and one of the voices that I heard was his, so I began to ask these voices to lead me to Skyler. I need you to know and understand these voices were demons. They began to lead me, and sure enough I pulled up at a hotel off of Estes Parkway and knocked on a random door, and a girl answered, and I asked, "Hey, is Skyler here?" "Yeah, let me go grab him for you," she said. I could not believe it. I found him by listening to voices in my head.

These voices that I heard only grew worse with the use of drugs. I could hear them when I was high, and I could hear them when I was not high. They usually disguised themselves as the voices of other people I knew. They would tear me down; they would mock me; they would play tricks on me and jokes on me. It was miserable. In today's world they would say that I had a mental disorder, but it was all the demons I had let in through sex and drugs and opening the door to the occult. I know what it is now, but at the time I thought maybe I just needed medication for schizophrenia.

There was a pretty rough hotel off Estes Parkway that I rented. We sat in that hotel for hours getting high, and I had some colors and a coloring book, and I was doing that…when the voices kicked in again and told me to go across the street to the Waffle House and kill myself. There were certain times when the voices knew things, so sometimes I would go with it, and this night I did. Without telling anyone, I just walked out of the front door and went to the Waffle House. I had a bag, but it didn't have a lot of stuff in it. When I got inside, I said, "Okay, now what…" The voices told me to walk in the bathroom, so I did. When I got in the bathroom, I said, "Okay, now what?" The voices said, "Take your charger out of your purse and hang yourself." I was so vulnerable and just oppressed by demons. I took my cell phone charger out of my bag and tried to make a noose out of it. I remember thinking that my parents and my kids would have a lot of questions, so before I placed myself in it, I called a close friend of mine who had been clean and doing really well. She and I were in prison together, but we stayed in close contact with each other, and I called her and said, "I think I am about to kill myself. I can't live like this anymore. I am so miserable, and I am at the Waffle House about to hang myself."

She made the right calls, and the police ended up coming and saving me once again. God's angels were on the move saving me from myself.

I should be dead. I know people throw that around loosely, but I, for real, should be dead, and I am grateful that heaven had another plan for me, and I am grateful that the Lord sends angels to minister to us and to strengthen us and to guard us in all our ways. My poor angels. I know I was a lot for them to protect.

The voices were getting louder and louder and always tricking me and tearing me down. I felt trapped, I felt ashamed, and I felt alone. I would try to outrun the voices, but they reached me in Gregg County Jail, they reached me in my parents' house, and they reached me in every hotel room. Those voices were not going anywhere. I had crossed the line. I had become one of those crazy people you see walking around whom you feel sorry for.

The devil never hands you a chain and says, "Here you go—wrap this around your neck and be bound by sin and addiction..." He is much more clever than that. He gives us one link at a time; each link is a choice, and once you make enough wrong choices, those links begin to form chains, and soon, over the course of time, you will become bound, and *only* Jesus Christ can break those chains. I don't say this to discourage you. I say this to encourage you to cry out to Jesus and ask Him to break those chains. Repent for the one link at a time and being deceived, and He will save you. It is extremely simple to say a prayer like, "Jesus, help me."

Skyler and I found a hotel on Highway 80 to set up at for a while. The hotel is called "The Palace Inn" and known for prostitution and drug use. I was still seeing Otto and the doctor on the side to get extra income. I would take the money and give it to Skyler as soon as I got it, and we would buy a week or two at hotels and use and sell drugs. We were robbing people, being robbed. We were in dangerous situations almost every weekend. My heart was hard, and my identity was a criminal; the voices in my head really made my flight or fight instinct kick in, so I was always on guard.

Brittany had been shot, and Skyler and I had been shot at, so there was no telling what was going to happen next. My sense of "doing right" had been seared. I was not faithful to Skyler. I was faithful to never leave his side, but I lied to him and did things behind his back, and I am sure he was doing the same type of things behind my back. We were toxic to one another. I came home from one of the times of being with the doctor and Skyler was in a terrible mood.

"We need to talk," he said. "Yeah. What's up?" I replied. "What exactly are you doing for this doctor?" he asked. I blew up. "I told you I am driving him and doing cleaning and cooking and just housekeeping stuff. I swear—why do you always charge me up about this? I am taking care of us, aren't I? I don't know what you want from me..."

"Yeah, well, I think you are having sex with them, and that is what the word on the street is, and I swear to God, Brittney, I am so tired of you cheating on me and lying to me..." he snapped back.

The truth is I was lying, and I was cheating, and I was not doing housework at the doctor's house, but I was so ashamed, I just could not admit it. We started fighting, and before you know it, things escalated very quickly, and he started spitting in my face and calling me horrible names. I just couldn't take it, so I left.

I started walking down Highway 80. I was so tired of living my life like this. I was so beaten down and broken. I just wanted to go to sleep. I found a place on the ground on some cement behind a restaurant, and I laid my head on the ground, and I went to sleep. As I fell asleep, I thought to myself, *I am sleeping outside on the ground. I am homeless. I am broken. I cannot believe my life started off so normal, and here I am...*

God was faithful. He sent his angels to arrest me and carry me to jail like clockwork. The enemy wanted to take my life, but God was not going to let me lose my life. He had a different plan for me.

I had been arrested eighteen times by the end of 2012, all because God was seeking me and trying to save that which was lost. Each time I was booked into jail, it was like being at home. I knew the routine. I would go into the trustee tank. I knew each day what was on the brown tray. I helped prepare the food; I sprayed and cleaned the trays; I read over the rosters, wrote some letters, and watched some TV, and I waited to be released and did the same old thing. One thing I did not do very often was go to church in Gregg County Jail. I did not want to be a hypocrite, and I felt like I had crossed over that line. I was one of the ones whom God wrote off and didn't really want anymore. I could write a book on all the crazy, wicked things that happened out on those streets and the supernatural hand of God saving me through police officers. At the time I thought they were my enemy. I hated them. I listened to songs about how terrible they were, but right now if you asked me my thoughts on the police, I would tell you the Lord uses them to save people from themselves. The police are amazing, and I am so grateful for them. I am grateful for the small role they played in my life and in saving me.

There was another night that I fully believe angels were dispatched from heaven to save me.

A guy who I thought was really handsome and had his stuff together asked me on a date. He was known around town for his family coming from money, and he drove a sports car, and I was only an acquaintance of his old girlfriend, so when he hit me up on Facebook messenger, I was surprised. He did drugs like me, but he was not nearly as deep into them as I was…so I thought. He came and picked me up, and I heard the sports car's engine rev a few times. Of course, I was staying in a hotel at the time. I came out to the car and jumped in. "Did you get your swimsuit like I said?" he asked me. "Yeah, I got it on right now; let's get out of here." Skyler and I were fighting, and I just wanted to get away. I was desperate to be in a different situation. Any situation besides the one I found myself in with Skyler. Little did I know I was about to be in a very dangerous situation. He pulled up to an apartment complex and said, "Okay, let's go swimming…" I remember jumping in the pool that night feeling some freedom I hadn't felt in a while. I was used to living in hotels, but here we were at a nice apartment complex. I swam around, but my arms were sore. I had been shooting for days, so to wave my arms under the water hurt. I got out and dried off, and even though it was dark outside, I lay out on the sunbathing chair, and I just relaxed. Brad came over to me and started asking me questions about life and love, and I thought to myself, *You know, this is really a step up from the way I have been living. I could get used to this.*

"You want to go for a ride?" "Sure, I'm down," I responded. We started driving down the highway and ended up at Lake Gladewater. It was dark outside, and this place was not somewhere I was super familiar with, and he was acting weird. The longer we sat there, the more scared I got. He wanted to get out of the car and walk through the woods, and something was telling me, "Don't do it," but I did. As we walked through the woods, he started acting super sketchy. I felt like he was going to hurt me. He was on and off his phone, and the more we walked, the worse the feeling in my gut got. He finally said he wanted to go back to the car and do some drugs, so I was relieved when I heard the bell ringing as I opened the passenger door and sat down. We got high, and then we went driving. We ended up at a hotel room. I could not shake the sketchy feeling inside that something wasn't right. Normally, when you come to a hotel room, you must check in; that is the first step, but he just drove straight up to the door and opened my door and said, "Come on." He looked sad; he looked upon me with despair, and I knew in my gut something was not right. When he opened the hotel room door, there were about five to six people inside. One of them had a mask on, and he was holding rope. He grabbed me and started to try to tie my feet up. Thank God I was so skinny because my arm slipped out of the hold that he tried to put me in, and I was able to break free. I shook the rope off my feet, and I ran faster than I had ever run in my entire life. I ran so far and so fast. I knew it; they were going to tie me up and hurt me. I called Skyler, and he was so angry. He could not believe it. I hid for what seemed like two hours, and he came and picked me up. He got on the phone and told everyone what these guys had done to me, and the word got out on the street, and we started looking for revenge. That was how we rolled. We got revenge. We were going to retaliate, and it would probably involve weapons and robbing them.

I was so scared on the way to rob these guys. We were five deep in two different vehicles. My crew, we were a ruthless crew and could be violent. Looking back, we were a bunch of insecure adults, running from God and addicted to substances. We had weapons, and we had masks. We heard that the house we were going to was full of drugs. That was really the only reason I was down. I was so nervous. I was scared I was going to get shot or arrested. Those were the two scenarios that played out in my mind the whole way there. When we pulled up, they sent me to the door. They knew they would open the door for me. My hand was so shaky as I knocked on the door. G came to it. His street name was "Gueto"; he was an up-and-coming dealer who was connected to Brad, the one who tried to kidnap me. "Hey, what's up, girl? Come in..." As soon as he opened the door enough for me to walk in, about eight people bum-rushed him, and we all stormed in the house. We started yelling that if everyone did what we said, nobody would get hurt. There were lots of girls there. I knew three of them, and they were cussing me out, saying, "How could you do this to us, Brittney? You set us up." We demanded they give us all the drugs. We got all the drugs and made everyone lay on the floor until we left. On the way home, I felt like the worst person in the world. I could not believe I just did that. The only thing that kept me feeling halfway okay about myself was that those men started all this the night they tried to kidnap me. It was really their fault. They picked this fight, and so what if we took some drugs? We didn't hurt anybody. We didn't shoot anybody. They would be okay if they didn't have those drugs. We got home, and I almost vomited when we walked in. I was sick at the person I had become. I was in deep now, too deep.

By the time 2013 rolled in, I had completely lost my mind to the darkness. I was actively hearing voices in my head and doing what they said no matter what state of mind I was in, but getting high made it worse. I was for real crazy, for real too far gone. I was getting further away from reality by the second. I was in a deep state of psychosis, and I had fortresses of lies in my mind that I believed. A lie that you believe can quickly become a stronghold in your mind, and that is exactly what I had. A ton of strongholds in my mind. To give you a kind of silly example, I believed that anyone who wore "Texas" gear was the feds. I believed that I was being watched by the feds and that I was in the middle of some kind of video game that was a conspiracy. I believed I was being set up to be murdered all the time. Not too long before I got clean, I had a friend give me a shot of dope, and I went into the bathroom and squirted in the sink because I thought he was trying to kill me. I called my dad that day to come pick me up and kept telling him, "They are trying to kill me. Please come pick me up. They are trying to kill me, Dad..."

My dad did pick me up that day at the Suburban Motel. I tried to explain to him what was going on in my head. He brought me home and let me shower and change clothes and eat something. I fell asleep on the couch that night, and the next morning I heard voices telling me to leave. I walked out that front door and started doing what they said again. It was like I was a puppet, being controlled by demons with no way to get out. No matter how loud I screamed, it was as if no one could hear me. Who could save me from myself? Christ, the Lord. He is the only way, He is the only truth, and He is the only life.

It felt a lot like *The Matrix*—the unexplainable things that would happen were like a glitch in the matrix. I remember walking down the road one day and having this thought in the spirit world that I was about to be shot at. Right when I heard the gun in my mind going off, I felt bullets in my back. I felt actual pain in my back like I was being shot. I remember thinking, *How in the world can this be real?* It really was like a video game. I knew I needed medication for my mental issues and probably mental illness, but God had something better in mind than medication. He wanted to heal me. He uses something way more powerful than any medication that you can take. He uses the blood of Jesus. Blood speaks a better word over you. He was beaten and bruised for our iniquities, and by His stripes we are *healed*. That is what the plan of heaven was for my mind. That was the plan to get me out of the matrix finally, once and for all. The blood of Jesus was the plan for me, and the blood of Jesus is the plan for you. Ephesians 2:13 (NIV):

"But now in Christ Jesus you who once were far away have been brought near by the blood of Christ."

Chapter 15

CHASING REBELS

I hope I won't need to show you when I come how harsh and rough I can be. I don't want to carry out my present plans against some of you who seem to think my deeds and words are merely those of an ordinary man. It is true that I am an ordinary, weak human being, but I don't use human plans and methods to win my battles. I use God's mighty weapons, not those made by men, to knock down the devil's strongholds. These weapons can break down every proud argument against God and every wall that can be built to keep men from finding him. With these weapons I can capture rebels and bring them back to God and change them into men whose hearts' desire is obedience to Christ. I will use these weapons against every rebel who remains after I have first used them on you yourselves and you surrender to Christ.

Second Corinthians 10:2–6 (TLB)

December 31st, 2013, was the day I died. This day was the beginning of the end for me; this was the day I was arrested for the twenty-first time and the *last* time. All the days I had lived led up to this day. My Independence Day. This was a crazy dark day for me, but also the day God would deliver His daughter and bring her into submission to Him. God loves chasing rebels down. I am convinced that being too far gone is just His type because that is exactly what He got with me. A woman who statistically and on paper would never make it but, when filled with His Spirit, would be a world changer.

One of my favorite things about being a Christian is reading the Bible and seeing that God uses broken people. There are so many people in the Bible who were jacked up and had issues, and God just used them anyway. Every issue you can imagine is right there between

Genesis and Revelation. There are all kinds of trauma—murder, incest, lust, greed—nothing new under the sun and *nothing* that Jesus can't heal. Jesus came from a bloodline of sinners just like us to save sinners just like us. God is so good. I always want my story to display the goodness of God. He delights in showing us mercy, and He loves to forgive us. He is a good God, slow to get angry, rich in compassion. He is just and fair and righteous.

It was freezing cold that night. I had been hanging out with Paul and Serinity all night. I was shivering in my black and gray peacoat holding my arms around me tightly because of how cold it was outside. I had a bad feeling in my gut. I can't explain it other than I knew something bad was going to happen. Ninety percent of the time I had an impending sense of doom and dread these days. My mind was a playground for the devil, so sensing doom was the norm for me, but this night was different... "I think we need to take communion..." I said to Serinity and Paul.

In case you don't know, communion is when you drink some sort of juice or wine as a representation of the blood of Jesus and you eat a small piece of bread, but before you eat it, you break it as a symbol that Jesus' body was broken for you and His blood was poured out. You remember Jesus when you do this. It sets your eyes on Him. It causes you to remember the body and the blood and what the Savior did for you. It is a time of reflection and looking upon the cross. To this day, I have no idea why it crossed my mind to do that, but I am sure that God has a reason.

"Communion?" They both looked at me like I was crazy. "Yeah, something bad is going to happen. I just know it. Maybe if we take communion and we drink the blood of Jesus and eat the body, Jesus will keep us safe or something. I don't know; I just feel like we are supposed to do it," I said.

This was the first time that I ever felt like I needed to take communion while I was using drugs. This was the first time that thought had ever come to my mind, but for whatever reason we did. I found some grape juice and crackers, and we stood there, the three of us circled up, and we ate our cracker and drank our juice, and I said some sort of prayer that Jesus would keep us safe. We had all been living a pagan lifestyle, but I had known Jesus at a young age, and dying was close for me; I just felt it. I was not going to be around much longer the way I was living, so I figured if I did that communion, maybe I would at least make it to heaven. I did not realize I was going to die that night, just not physically. God was going to bring me to the end of myself, just not the way I necessarily wanted it to happen.

Paul was the only one out of the three of us that had a vehicle, and he fell asleep... We had been getting high all night, so for him to fall asleep was so weird to me. I thought he was faking it. How in the world could he sleep under the influence of what we were on? It did not make sense. I remember I put my face as close as I could to his, and I said, "Are you faking it?" He was just as still as he could be, then I yelled, "*Faking it...*" He did not respond at all. I had a crazy idea because I was full of those. I looked at Serenity. "Hey...let's take his car while he is asleep..." I said. "No, I don't think we should do that, " she responded back very low under her breath. "Come on, let's get out of here. That is our only way out. I will very gently get the keys out of his pockets while he sleeps...I will take them; you don't have to do anything..."

Serenity 100 percent did not trust me, and it showed. I don't know if it was the communion or what, but she almost seemed scared of me doing something crazy. She was right about me. I was a liar, a manipulator, and the most selfish human. But she and Paul were not much better. Most people on the street and on drugs are selfish human beings.

I put my knee down on my bed and extended my arm toward Paul's blue jeans. He was snoring, so I knew he was in a pretty deep sleep. I so gently stuck my hand in his front left pocket and began fishing around for the keys. I found them, but I couldn't pull them out because the pants were so tight. I pulled my hand back and took a deep breath and tried again. I got the keys the second time; I looked at Serinity, and she shook her head. "Let's go," I said. It took Serinity a few minutes to come with me. She knew what this meant. We were stealing a car, and she wasn't as excited as I was. At this point, I had been arrested twenty times, and I was used to breaking the law. My conscience was seared.

I started the car as quickly as I could because it was freezing outside. My heart was pounding. I could not believe I was stealing a car. I had really let myself get out there badly. We burnt out of the trailer park Paul lived in, and we started driving. I had nowhere to go, but the voices in my head were telling me to go look for Skyler. They were saying to find him, and that is what I was going to do—find Skyler. Skyler and I had pretty much split up, but there was still an unhealthy soul tie that had not been broken, so even if we weren't together, I looked for him because, in my mind, he loved me and accepted me for who I was; he never turned me away. We just couldn't keep a roof over our heads together. We couldn't feed both of our addictions. When we first met, he had a very healthy appetite for drugs, and mine was minor compared to his, but after we were together, my appetite was just as strong as his, and there was no way to feed both; somebody was going to starve, and it wasn't going to be him, and it sure wasn't going to be me, so we split and just tried to live apart, but I still loved him, and I still thought about it a lot.

Serinity told me that she wanted me to make a stop in Gladewater. I asked her for directions, and she told me. I started heading toward the house she asked me to go to. When we pulled in, Serinity looked at me right in my eyeballs and said, "Brittney, *promise me* you won't leave me here. You aren't leaving, are you?" "No, no, I won't leave you," I responded. She said, "Please don't." I said, "No, I am just going to wait right here in the car."

Serinity got out of the car, and I watched her in the rearview mirror. As soon as she was far enough away from the car and she had no chance of getting back in, I burnt out on her. I put my foot to the pedal and sped off as fast as I could. I bet I left tire marks on the asphalt because I heard the screech of the tires and the engine revving as I sped away. I could not take her on this trip with me because, truth be told, I had no idea what reality or universe I was in. I was in some kind of game listening to voices in my head and those voices told me to speed off and leave her in the dust, and that is exactly what I was doing. Little did I know, there were over five grams of methamphetamine in the glovebox that either Serinity or Paul had in there. I wish I had known that because my crazy hiney would have tried to do it, but I was naive to it. I really didn't know it was in there. I would find out soon enough though, just not the way I wanted.

I got on I-20 and started driving all over Longview, Gladewater, Kilgore, just driving and driving, listening to the voices in my head. Water started to sprinkle on the windshield of the car, and it seemed like as the day went on, it was getting colder and rainier and just more foggy and gross outside. Sleet was starting to fall on the windshield instead of rain. To this day, I do not know how all of it happened, but I ended up somewhere in Upshur County in the woods in a giant mud pit. I was stuck in the mud in the middle of nowhere. I started panicking when the silver SUV's tires were just spinning. There was no getting out, but I gave it my best try! I got out of the SUV and started trying to push it and trying to put sticks under the tires so I would have enough traction to move, but it did not work. I was in the mud, and I had mud all over me.

There are several scriptures about mud and mire in the Bible and God rescuing us from the mud. In Luke 15 we see the prodigal son in the mud with the pigs; it was while he was in the mud that the prodigal "came to his senses" and thought to himself that he should go back to his father's house. Perhaps God must allow us to get into the mud to come to our senses.

The next thing I remember is hearing sirens coming closer and closer to my location. When the police pulled in, they asked me what

I was doing out there, and I don't remember exactly what I told them, but I do remember them finding the dope, needles, and paraphernalia and putting handcuffs on me and taking me to Upshur County Jail.

I was booked into jail barely alive and barely in reality. I honestly just wanted to die. I remember hearing voices in my mind saying, "Just kill yourself; your kids deserve better than this. How many times now have you been arrested? You are nothing but a junkie and piece of crap. Just get it over with and kill yourself."

Most of the time, I could fight through these feelings of hopelessness and suicide, but I had been fighting it for eleven long years. I was tired of fighting it. I, *for real*, was going to kill myself as soon as I had the opportunity. I was just going to get it over with, and the earth and everyone in it would be better off if I was gone. I believed that. I could not get it together no matter how hard I tried. I had mud all over my body when I was booked into jail. Everyone there was asking me why I had mud on me, and I was trying to explain it the best I could. I had tried to hide the dope on my person, but, of course, a wonderful Christian lady searched me, and, boom, God revealed it. She found the dope. I tried to tell her it wasn't mine, but it was on my person, so I took the charge for it. I needed to eat, and I needed to sleep. I took a shower and ate something and went to sleep for what felt like several days. When I woke up, I remember hearing a voice call out, "Time for church! Do any of you ladies want to go to church?" and for whatever reason, my body got up off my bunk and got in line for church.

I walked into a room within the jail, and there were about five other inmates there with me. We began to sing the silliest worship songs like "Jesus Loves Me" and "This Little Light of Mine." I was not feeling it. I crossed my arms across my chest and thought to myself, *Man, these people have no idea who I am and what I am capable of.*

A nice lady named Janice Easly got up to preach. There were two volunteers that night, Joyce and Janice. They were both sweet ladies, but they had no idea how broken I was. I sat there with a hardened heart and a seared conscience, but I listened to her preach.

I was fascinated by Janice; there was something about her that was glorious. She was a beautiful lady; she was well put together with nice clothes, and her face was pretty, and her eyes were just so full of light and life. She was preaching about how God brought her out of the same type of things I was involved in, and then she started saying, "God sent me here tonight; I have been praying in the Spirit, and I have been seeing something in the Spirit, and I want you to know..." She locked eyes with me. "God wants *you* to know...that He was *right there with you while you were trapped in that mud...*"

When she said the word "mud," something broke. She was staring right into my soul, and the anointing of God was so strong on her, and I just broke. I began to weep. How could she know that I was in that mud pit? Was God really seeing me right now? It felt like the doors of my chest just flung open, and God was standing there in front of me, staring right into my heart.

She knew that she had struck something inside of me; she was standing there staring right into my eyes, and no matter how badly I wanted her to break the glare, she would not back down. I was hoping she would just go away and keep preaching, but God was speaking to her, and He was speaking to her about *me*, and she was being obedient to minister to me at that moment. God can change *everything* in a single moment. The whole trajectory of my life changed in this simple five-second moment.

"Do you want to go to the throne of *grace* where you can obtain mercy from the Lord and receive forgiveness for your sins?" she asked me so gently.

"Yes," I shakily responded. "Okay, come here, and I am going to pray for you." She began to pray, and faith started rising in me. I didn't want to live like this anymore. Deep, deep down I wanted to get my life back on track with the Lord, so I prayed, and I asked God to forgive me. I told Him that I was sorry for running from Him and, please, to give me another chance. I was exactly like the prodigal son. I had come to my senses in the middle of that mud, and I wanted to go home to the Father. I wanted Him to forgive me and give me another chance.

God's mercy and grace had been chasing me for a long long time, and it finally caught up with me because I finally was at the end of myself. I had lost my mind, I had lost peace, I had lost so much, and I was so tired of losing. I was so tired of hurting. I was spiritually starving. I had landed on my knees. The world that I had been living in up until this point had crumbled. It was not a safe place for me. I was ready to burn it all down. I was ready to lay everything down at the feet of Jesus. I found myself needing someone to save me. I needed a Savior. I needed a best friend. I needed a deliverer; I needed a father.

The prodigal son had just started down the road to return to his father, and his father saw him coming from a long way away, and his father ran to him. One of the first lessons I learned from this story is that God runs. Did you know that God runs? In this story that Jesus is telling about the prodigal son; the father in the story is a representation of God. He ran to his son and embraced Him. He was waiting for him to return and looking for him to return. Perhaps God is waiting on *you*. Perhaps you need to get out of the pig pen you have been in and take that first step to return home to your Father. Perhaps you need to make a choice to turn around and land right smack in the middle of the most loving Father you could ever imagine. I encourage you right now. Let God father you. Maybe a big part of what is going on with you is you didn't have a dad, or you had a deadbeat dad, or you had an abusive dad who treated you badly. God is not like that. He is the best Father you could ever imagine, and the fact that He is waiting for you and He put this book in your hand is proof of His great love for you. You would not even be reading it right now if He was not trying to reach you. He loves you. He wants you to come home, child. He wants to forgive you and cover all that shame and guilt with his love and mercy.

I got back to my jail cell that night, and I knelt in front of my bunk. "God, I am so sorry. I know You love me. I know You sent that lady to tell me that You were there with me in the mud. I want to serve You for the rest of my life. My life is such a mess, and it is *so* broken, but You can have it; if You can do something with it, here it is. I lay down everything, and I completely surrender to You being the Lord in my life. Nothing I am doing is working; I need You. I need You to be the Lord, and I will just obey what You say. Please help me. Amen."

I slept like a baby that night. I felt a peace in my soul that could not be explained. When I woke up the next morning, the most amazing thing happened. For eleven years I had heard voices. I knew I was a little crazy and I would probably need medicine to not hear voices, but the next day the evil voices were gone. It was a real-life miracle. My mind was back. My peace was back. I was a new person. I was born again.

The only thing I heard was the most beautiful voice, and this is what it said to me, "Brittney, I love you. You are My daughter, and I am so pleased you came home to Me. From this day forward, I am going to speak to you. I am going to take *all* the evil things that were intended to harm you, and I am going to use them for your good, so you will hear My voice now, and you will use it for My glory."

Wow, this was amazing. "Does anybody have a Bible?" I said out loud in the jail cell. "I have one," one of the girls responded. I needed to read the Bible; I just felt that in my soul. If I was going to be a Christian, I needed a Bible.

I will never forget the first thing I read in the Bible. I just randomly flipped it open somewhere in the middle, and the words jumped off the page straight inside of me. "The Sovereign Lord has filled me with his Spirit. He has chosen me and sent me To bring good news to the poor, To heal the broken-hearted, To announce release to captives And *freedom to those in prison*" (Isaiah 61:1, GNT). *Whoa, that is amazing. God could totally get me out of this prison*, I thought to myself. The Bible is amazing. You don't read it ever. It reads *you*; it is alive, and it has a heartbeat, and it is the most powerful and amazing book/person I have ever experienced. I held on to that scripture and to that word from God like it was an actual promise and prophetic word over my life. I began to hear God say, "I am going to release you, Brittney. I am setting you free on the inside first, and then you are going to physically walk out of this jail." How could this be? I had a stack of felonies as long as my arm. Naturally this was impossible, but somehow, I just believed what God was saying. If He was speaking it, I believed it. I had this crazy childlike faith that just believed everything the Lord was telling me. It was such an amazing transformation happening on the inside of me! It was a moment that changed everything; the entire trajectory of my life was *changed* in an instant. I knew in my heart that I would never be the same again. It was a radical change.

    It was not all lollipops and rainbows; I had been addicted to drugs for years, so the first thing that happened was I broke out in hives *all* over my body. I went to the doctor, and he could not figure out what it was. They tried different medicines and different creams, but the hives stayed; nothing really helped except reading my Bible. I would lie there in my bunk in jail and read and read, and sometimes my heart would start pounding, and I would feel intense anxiety, but I would hear God whisper, "Just keep reading, Brittney—keep going, keep fighting..." And I would. I would grip the pages in my hands so tight sometimes because the hives would be itchy, and I would feel so much anxiety, but I would set my face like *flint* to the pages. I would not back down. I was all in. There was no disease, no demon, no anxiety that could keep me from the Word of God. It was as if the Word was healing me and setting me free. One time I even saw the words sort of coming off the pages in my mind and going on assignments to accomplish what it was sent forth to do.

I remember telling the Lord I wasn't going to watch the TV in our tank at *all* unless it glorified Him. I would read my Bible from the minute I woke up until the minute I closed my eyes to sleep. I was for real *all in*; I was never going back to the woman I used to be. I had been born again. My faith was so crazy during this time. I honestly would not have been surprised if an angel of the Lord appeared to me and the foundations of the jail shook and the angel just led me out of jail. That is how radical my faith was. I remember just being like, "Okay, God, let's do this, whatever it looks like." There is nothing greater than a sinner returning home. The Bible says that *all* of heaven rejoices. Heaven must have had a *big* party for me because I was a *big* sinner who had finally come to repentance. There is no greater feeling than being born again. I was so full of love for everyone and everything. I just loved everything again. The hate was gone. The confusion was gone. The demons were gone. This was what it meant to be alive. You could have told me that I was going to receive a life sentence, and I would have been okay with it. I had found life and what it meant. My whole life felt like a search for truth and joy and peace, and finally I had the source of all those things, and the crazy thing is He was there all along. Isn't it interesting how in *The Wizard of Oz* the characters were searching for something within themselves the whole time? Do you need courage? It is in you. Do you need strength? You can find it within you. Do you need peace, love, joy? Perhaps you are searching for something that is already there. I say it is within you because, as a Christian, I believe that I have been crucified with Christ, and it is no longer I who lives but Christ who lives *in me*. If Christ is *in me*, then I have everything I need! I need nothing. He is everything. If I had Him, I would have everything. If I did not have Him, I would have nothing. It is as simple as that. I believe that is what Paul meant when he said, "I can do all things through Christ who strengthens me" (Philippians 4:13, NKJV). I can be in immense suffering and pain, I can be beaten, I can be thrown in prison, but none of these things can take Christ from me, the hope of glory.

Chapter 16

BAD NEWS COMES FIRST

> *Now therefore fear the Lord and serve him in sincerity and in faithfulness. Put away the gods that your fathers served beyond the River and in Egypt, and serve the Lord. And if it is evil in your eyes to serve the Lord, choose this day whom you will serve, whether the gods your fathers served in the region beyond the River, or the gods of the Amorites in whose land you dwell. But as for me and my house, we will serve the Lord.*
>
> Joshua 24:14–15 (ESV)

Often in life, bad news comes first. I was in Upshur County Jail, and I had made a radical decision for the Lord, but it did not spare me from heartache. When you make a decision for the Lord, *often* bad news comes first. The Lord invites us to come to Him, to be with Him in the good times and in the bad times, and He promises to comfort us in the bad times and to help us through the hard things.

I would turn my back to the TV that was in my tank. The devil would try to mock me and speak to me through secular shows on TV, so I remember just thinking, *I will just turn my back on it, and then it won't affect me.* This turned out to be a powerful display of my love for Jesus. I would wake up early, turn my back to the TV, and study and read my Bible for hours. Oh, how I began to fall in love with the Word of God. I absolutely loved reading the Bible. It was feeding me, and it was literally like medicine to my sick soul; it was healing me from the inside out. It was also cleansing me. My thoughts for eleven years were so perverted and distorted, but as I read the Word of God, a deep cleansing was happening in my mind. Like a warm, soapy luffa just cleaning my mind as I would flip the pages in the Bible and read more and more.

"Brittney Major...come get these court papers at the gate," the guard said. When she first called my name, I thought, *Eeeek, this is* it. *I am about to get out of here. God is opening the doors of the jail and setting me free* just *like He said He would.*

I went to the gate to get the papers as quickly as I could. "These here are papers from a lawyer that state they are going to terminate your rights to your children," the guard gently explained to me.

I very slowly walked back to my bunk and flipped through the pages. The words jumped off the pages, "Terminate right to children, abandoned children for more than six months, drug use, extensive criminal history..." *Man, this is not good*, I thought to myself. I sat on my bunk, and I had a sinking feeling in my gut; it was over for me and my relationship with my kids. I kind of knew this was coming. I was a terrible mother to them, and they deserved so much better than me, and now they would have it. I put the papers under my pillow, and I pulled my blanket tightly over my whole body and my head, and I began a deep, ugly cry. I mourned. Just like they were dead, I mourned, and it was not pretty; the other five women in my tank knew to leave this one alone and to not say a word to me. This was deep emotional pain I was experiencing; there was no consoling me. There was no comforting me. This one hurt badly.

I was shocked. I could not believe it. How could God do this to me? After the choice I just made, I thought good things were supposed to happen. I was absolutely crushed. My heart hurt physically. I felt like I couldn't breathe. I felt like I was at a funeral for my children. I was confused. I thought when you became a Christian, good things happened, and you were spared from this sort of grieving. Initially, I wanted to give up. I was thinking, *Well, should I go back out to the streets and to drugs?* Then I remembered something that I prayed for after that church service. I remembered saying to God, "I am going to serve You the rest of my life." I had to do that. I had to follow through with my commitment, so again I went before the Lord. I said, "God, this hurts so badly; I do not want to lose my kids, but I trust You. I trust You, and if You think it's best that I don't be a mother to my children, that's okay with me, but, please, Lord, if You could work it out, I don't want to lose my babies." Maverick and Maci had just turned three, and Madisyn was ten at the time. I could see their little faces in my mind. I wanted so badly to see the change in me and to see what God did in my life. I am convinced that this is how God works sometimes. He is not concerned with your comfortability nearly as much as He is concerned with your character. Who are you when things don't go your way? You can say you are all in all you want, but are you really? Are you all in when things don't go your way and you are crushed? That was the challenge for me as I cried and read through these termination papers.

As I lay there that day crying, I remember God saying, "Go back to the Bible, open your Bible, and read it." I got up and opened my Bible randomly again, and you would not believe the words that I read. The words that I read said, "The Sovereign LORD says to his people: 'I will signal to the nations, and they will *bring your children home*'" (Isaish 49:22, GNT). Wow, what a promise. I just knew in my heart that it was going to be okay, and I remember just standing on that verse and saying, "Okay, God, this looks one way, but You can turn it all around, and if Your Word says it, then I believe it. You are going to bring my children home. Someway, somehow, I am not going to lose my kids. I trust You, and I believe in You, God." I could not wait to get back to church. I needed to talk to Janice Easly about all of this and get some advice. I would have a court date soon, and I needed wisdom.

They finally called church again. I had been waiting a couple of days, so I was ready when they called it. When I saw Janice, I ran up to her and said, "Janice, they are wanting to send me to prison for ten years, and I got papers to terminate my rights to my children…I am so scared. I don't know what to do." She looked at me and smiled; she said, "You need to fast and pray, honey, and you need to believe in God for a miracle." That same day the guards came in and let us go to the library. As I was looking at the bookshelf and trying to pick out a book to read, my eyes skimmed across all the old books and the wooden shelf, and I locked my eyes to a book because it said the very words that Janice said to me—right there in front of me was a book called *Fasting*. I grabbed it, and as soon as I got back to my bunk, I opened it, and I made up my mind. *I am going to read this book, and I am going to fast and pray and believe God for a miracle.*

Chapter 17

THE WAITING

"But those who hope in the Lord will renew their strength. They will soar on wings like eagles and they will run and not grow weary, they will walk and not be faint."

Isaiah 40:31 (NIV)

The first meeting I had with my lawyer, he did not hold anything back. "You are going to prison," he told me. "They have a lot of evidence on you, and there is no way they are going to give you probation. As of today, the state is offering you ten years, so you might as well sign for it and get on down the road to prison so you can get out," he explained. "I know you are going to think I am crazy, sir, but in Isaiah 61 the Bible says that God will set the prisoner free, and I just really think He is going to let me out of this jail cell. I know that sounds crazy, but I just believe that is what God is saying to me." He looked at me like I needed to be in the loony bin instead of jail or prison, but he responded with, "Look, these are the choices you made, and you are going to have to pay for them." "I understand what you are saying; I am just saying that God is speaking to me in this jail cell, and I truly believe that He is going to set me free, so I am sorry, but I cannot sign for that ten years today." I did not sign, and they took me back to my cell, but I knew that was the offer on the table.

As I was waiting for my next court date, I began to read that book on fasting. The first thing the book teaches you is that "King Stomach" runs the show most of the time, and it is very difficult to tell him no. The book recommended an "easy does it" approach; in other words, do not fast every meal and drink only water for thirty days when you first start fasting. I decided that for my first fast I would fast bread and sweets. The book *Fasting* is based on the scripture, "Though one may be overpowered, two can defend themselves. A cord of three strands is not quickly broken" (Ecclesiastes 4:12). The book said that fasting and praying and giving are the three cord strands that cannot be easily broken, so that is what I did. I started with a small fast like no meat, then I would move into heavier fasting like a Daniel fast with no sweets or meat or bread.

    I would also mix fasting with giving and with prayer. I would turn my back to the TV in my tank, and I would read my Bible. I would also watch *a lot* of Christian TV. We had cable, so I would watch TBN, and it would minister to my heart. TBN was a huge part of teaching me about the Lord. I would watch every show and take notes on the scriptures that the pastors and teachers taught on. TBN taught me how to be a Christian; TBN built my faith and stirred up the gifts inside of me. I remember wanting to be on TBN one day to give my testimony. I had never been in a jail where you could access TBN before; it was such a huge blessing to be able to be mentored and taught through the TV. Thank You, Jesus, that this jail had TBN in it. I do not know if I would be the person I am today without those profound teachings I learned in that jail cell.

    Fasting in jail is hard. The only way to fill the emptiness that you feel in your heart is with food, so food is a big deal there, but I would give mine away, and I would be so hungry, but I would just pray and read my Bible anytime I felt hungry. The longer I did this, the more God delivered me. There is a scripture in the Bible where the disciples are trying to cast out a demon, and Jesus says, "This one can only come out with prayer and fasting" (Matthew 17:21, NKJV). Jesus delivered me from all demons in that jail cell. There was nothing that was impossible for me. I was ministering to other ladies and giving them my time, reading scriptures. It did not matter if my whole world would have crumbled; I was on a solid foundation of Jesus Christ, and I could not be shaken. It was amazing!

    It was truly an experience that is hard to put words on. I felt closer to God than I ever knew possible. It was like He was just talking to me like an old friend. I could not get enough of Him. I wanted

Him so close; I wanted His voice in my ear; I wanted His guidance and direction more than I wanted food. There was nothing like His friendship; when I was with Him, I just felt alive and safe on the inside. I loved His presence.

The second time I went to court, I was expecting it to be the day God set me free, but they offered me a little worse offer than the first time. The first offer was ten years TDC; the second offer was ten years TDC plus Bowie County Women's Treatment Center after prison. Again, I went before the court and my lawyer sounding like a crazy person saying that I had an encounter with God and that He was speaking to me and I truly believed He was going to set me free. Again, I got all the crazy looks and glances and laughs under the breath, but I didn't care. I had a fire inside of me that could never be quenched. I was on fire for God, and nothing or no one could ever take from me what God had freely given me.

My lawyer was a nice man, but he was pressuring me to sign the second time. He told me the offer was not going to be any better and if I didn't sign that day, I would have to sign the next time I went to court. I told him I would take my chances.

I had one more chance. I got very serious about the Lord and about the fasting, praying, and giving. I was not going to miss what God was doing. I was diligent and intentional when it came to time in my Word. I listened to a lot of sermons, and I sang. The main song I sang said:

> *Jesus, you are the lover of my soul. Jesus, I will never let you go. You have taken me from the miry clay, set my feet upon a Rock, and now I know that I love you. I need you. Though my world will fall I will never let you go. My Savior. My closest friend, I will worship you until the very end.*

That is an old song, probably from the '90s, but, man, that was the song on my heart.

I sang that over and over because that was my story. He took me out of that mud, and He set my feet upon the rock, and I truly sincerely loved Jesus for it. I loved Him so much for giving me another chance. I did not deserve it, but He so freely gave it.

The doors in our tank were loud, so when they opened and closed, it made a loud noise. I was trying to sleep one night, and I heard the doors shut. When I opened my eyes, I saw a young lady standing in front of me. She looked broken and sad, and she was talking to herself under her voice. Her hair was sticking straight up like she had been electrocuted, and her pants were hanging way down like she was "sagging." She was probably crazy like I was when I first came to this place. I had compassion for her. I knew what it was like to lose your kids and lose your mind and be so trapped and controlled by the devil. I had seen God; I had beheld His glory, and it ruined me. I was overwhelmed by Him and the depths of His love. The Bible says, "Taste and see that the Lord is good" (Psalm 34:8, NIV). That is exactly what I had done. I had tasted and seen, and I *knew* He was good, and I prayed for this girl coming into the tank.

The next morning, when I woke up, I decided I was going to give that girl some stuff. I really felt like that was what the Lord wanted me to do. After all, I was fasting, praying, and giving. This was a part of giving—you had to find someone to give to! She was perfect because she had just arrived and she didn't have anything. I kept all my personal items under my mattress, so I went to my bunk and flipped my mattress up and began to make this girl a care package. I had been there for a while, so I had acquired a lot of stuff from all of the inmates who had been in and out. I put everything that I was going to give her on the left side of the mattress, and I put everything I was keeping for myself on the right side of the mattress.

I put her a couple of pairs of underwear and a T-shirt, a little bit of shampoo and conditioner, and a few more hygiene items, and I put all of the things I was going to give her in a towel, and I wrapped the towel up and threw it over my shoulder like Santa Claus and began to take it to her. As I was walking to her bunk, I heard the Lord say, "Stop, Brittney. Turn around. I want you to give her everything that you were going to keep for yourself, and I want you to keep the towel and the care package that you prepared for her." I stopped dead in my tracks. This was a radical statement from the Lord because I had *a lot* of stuff. I heard what He said, and I obeyed. I did as He told me, and I gave her a whole mattress fitted sheet *filled* with stuff, and I kept the little towel with the few items in it.

I did not sleep well that night—probably because I had given away all my stuff and I didn't have a pillow anymore. I was a little stirred in my spirit. I began to think, *I might actually lose my kids and spend the next ten years in prison...* I was okay with that, but the reality of it was starting to set in, and I was beginning to think maybe I didn't hear God as clearly as I thought I had, but I just kept hearing God say, "I am going to set you free." I wrestled with those extremes that night, and eventually I put my hand on my heart, and I asked God, "Father, speak truth to my heart."

Chapter 18

FREEDOM

> *"The Spirit of the Lord is on me, because he has anointed me to proclaim good news to the poor. He has sent me to proclaim freedom for the prisoners and recovery of sight to the blind, to set the oppressed free."*
>
> Luke 4:18 (NIV)

My final court date came quickly. I had been fasting and praying for ninety-two days, and I had spent time with the Lord all morning on the day of my final court date. I was nervous, but at the same time, I had peace. I had a girl braid my hair, and I brushed my teeth and pinched my cheeks so I could have a little color in my face. I was ready. No one knew how hungry I was and how I had been fasting. They didn't know because I was so happy. The Bible says when you fast, you should not look sad and miserable like the hypocrites, but you should put oil on your face and look happy! And your Father who sees what is done in private will reward you for it. My private life was completely for the Lord, and I believed that scripture. I had no secrets, I had no shame, and I had no guilt. The blood of Jesus had washed over me and washed all my sins away. The new had come, and the old had washed away. I had longed for love for so long. I knew I was going to court, but no matter the outcome, I was a changed and new and different woman than the woman who had booked into that jail. I could feel the Lord smiling down on me, and it didn't matter what happened in court, I was loved and accepted by the Father—nothing else mattered.

When I walked in the courtroom, my lawyer was on the side of the table where I sat, but when I looked across to where the DA normally sat, there was a different person there. My lawyer said, "Brittney, let's go over in this room on the side and talk for a few minutes." I followed him, shackled at my hands and my feet, remembering the word God had spoken over me that He would set the captives free.

I sat at the table, and my lawyer sat across from me. He had some papers in his hand, and he slid them across the table to me. "The prosecutor that was on your case dropped it this morning, and a new prosecutor got assigned to it, and I can't believe I am even telling you this, but they are offering you four years' probation today, and you are going to get out of jail *today*."

Right then and right there, I dropped to my knees, and I said, "Thank You, Jesus…thank You for setting me free. You are the truth, and You are the way, and You are life. I acknowledge You right here and right now. *You* have done this. You have torn down these prison walls, and You have set Your daughter free, and I will never forget it."

I acknowledged God in the moment, I turned my head to heaven, and I said, "God, I *know* You did this. Just like You said You would!"

When we honor God, God honors us. I think too often we get so busy in life that we forget to even acknowledge the Lord! We just go about our day like He doesn't even exist. Like we can just do life without Him. Nonsense, the truth couldn't be further. We cannot even speak without Him or move without Him. Without Him we are nothing. Sometimes I say, "Here we are just spinning on this green and blue ball in outer space…" How does this ball spin? How do we not burn up because we are too close to the sun? Or freeze to death because we are too far away from the sun? *The Lord is why.* He keeps us in perfect rotation, He holds that ball in His hands, and He sees fit to give us the breath in our lungs. We need to thank Him more for the perfection of the earth and everything in it, for the plan and the purpose He has for our lives. Who is like the Lord? No one.

I could not sign those papers fast enough. After they were signed, my lawyer explained to me that I would still have to go and stand before the judge for probation. I had never been to Upsher County Jail before. Like I mentioned before, this was my twenty-first time being arrested, and the first twenty times were in Gregg County, so this was my first time to go before this judge. She was a woman, and

I was a little scared to stand in front of her. I was thinking, *Oh man, I hope she doesn't change her mind...I hope she doesn't look back over my record and say, "Wait a minute—we can not go through with this; her record is too extensive, and there is no way she is going to complete this probation."* Instead of the judge being harsh like I had pictured in my mind, when I stood in front of her, she was almost gentle when she spoke these words to me from the stand, "Brittney, you are being given an opportunity to change your life today, and I really hope you do, but if I ever see you in this courtroom again, I promise you will go to prison for ten years flat. I am not playing with you." I did not take that lightly. I knew she meant business, but deep down I knew I would never be back in the courtroom again! This was it for me. Heaven was going to help me. God was going to empower me and strengthen me, and I was never going to be the same. I didn't know a lot, but I knew that.

The game was over. I had heaven on my side now. I had God on my side. I was confident that God was going to finish this work that he had started in me. I was confident that I would never be back in jail—I would never stand with handcuffs on my wrist being sentenced by a judge ever again. I was forgiven, I was free, and I was able to say goodbye to all the past and really move forward.

That day marked me forever. It was a real-life miracle. It was also a prophecy fulfilled. I first opened my Bible that day to *"He will set the prisoner free,"* and now here I was about to walk out of the jail. It is so much better this way. For so many years, I thought that life had to be a certain way, but there is a better way. Life can be so beautiful and miraculous and just wonderful when you give the broken pieces to Jesus when you just tell Him, "Look—I have made a mess of my life, but if You can do something with it, here it is."

Chapter 19

YOU GOTTA START SOMEWHERE

> *"Brothers and Sisters, I do not consider myself yet to have taken hold of it. But one thing I do: forgetting what is behind and straining toward what is ahead."*
>
> Philippians 3:13 (NIV)

I got released that very day to probation. I did not have anywhere to go; I was going to tell my probation officer that I wanted to go to some kind of women's program if they would allow me to. I walked into Chris Brown's office a little high on freedom. I could not wipe the smile from my face. I sat down in front of him and explained to him that I had been living on the streets for a long time and making money illegally and that I really didn't have a home. I told him that I had great parents, but they were done with my crap, and they had actually served me papers while in jail to terminate my right to my children, so I had that court date coming up. I told him there was no way my parents were going to let me back home. I remember him looking at me and sort of smiling. "Are you sure about that? Your parents want nothing to do with you?" I responded, "Oh yes, sir, they are done. I have really hurt them." He said, "Well, would it surprise you if your dad is on his way to pick you up right now? And they have agreed to give you another chance? They have agreed to cancel those termination papers if you are for real about these changes, and you do good, and you stay clean?"

I could not believe it. *Another word* that God spoke over me was being fulfilled in front of my very eyes. I was not going to lose my kids; my parents were going to give me another chance. Miracle after miracle, "Thank You, Jesus," were the only words that felt right, even though the weight of those words coming out of my mouth did not seem enough. He will bring my children home from afar. God was the most amazing person I had ever encountered; He is the only One with power to change you and your life.

I had nothing. I had the shirt on my back and the jacket I was wearing the night I was arrested and one pair of jeans. *All* my belongings had been confiscated because of the nature of my charge and it being a drug charge. I had no glasses, I had no jewelry, my clothes were muddy, the police confiscated everything, but you want to hear something profound? The police had taken everything from me, but when I booked into jail, they gave me *one* thing, and that one thing was a Bible. *In* other words, they took *everything*, but all of that was rubbish. Isn't that amazing? I had *nothing*, no possessions, but I had everything, and I was rich because I had Christ! Wow, what an exchange. To be honest I would do it all over again. Everything in this world is rubbish compared to knowing Christ. He is all you will ever need. Only He satisfies.

I moved back into my parents' house. I became humble like a servant. I had no cell phone. I had nothing. I just did what they did and followed them around like a puppy for the first few months. I took care of my babies. I got my babies back.

The night I was arrested I had lost my wallet. Somewhere in the mix I had left it at a drug dealer's house tucked in the couch. I remember tucking it in the couch, and I remember leaving it there. So I knew I would have to get an ID and all the things you must do when you lose a wallet. At the time my dad owned a car dealership. I was there with him one day, and he asked me to clean out this gold minivan. I went out there and started taking everything out of it so I could prepare it to wash, dry, and vacuum it and everything to get it clean for my dad. When I was in the middle of doing this, I looked down, and I saw a card face down by itself in the middle aisle of the van. I picked it up, and it was my ID. I began crying because I knew it was impossible for this to happen, and so gently I heard the Lord say, "You have found your true identity, Brittney; this is who you are, and you have finally found it. Now you must never look back."

I ran in the car lot, and I said, "Mom...Dad...how did y'all get my ID in that van? How did this happen? I just found my ID in that van." They had no idea how it got there, but my mom said, "Maybe God did that, Brittney; maybe it was a miracle." It had to have been.

Miracle after miracle after miracle... A lot of people are searching for a miracle. Maybe all we really need to do is go look in the mirror; perhaps we are the miracle. Perhaps the gift of Jesus to save us and change us and make us new people is exactly the type of miracle we are looking for.

I started looking for work soon after I got out. I had been arrested twenty-one times, so I knew it was going to be difficult to find a job. I found one at a place called "The Popcorn Gallery." I made popcorn and candy and ended up working there for a Christian lady. I made $7.25 an hour. Listen, you must start somewhere. When you are first starting your life over, you cannot just start at the top. You must learn to trust God in the process of refining you and renewing your mind. I tell people all the time, "Just start somewhere!" Even if it is at McDonald's or whatever! Be faithful in whatever you are doing, and He will lead you, guide you, and take you from glory to glory.

I also spent a lot of time with the Lord. I had a little section of my room that was my prayer room, and I would go in there every night and talk to the Lord. I love the Lord so much. One of my favorite promises in the Bible is that when we seek Him, we *find* Him. Isn't that amazing? All we must do is seek Him, and He promises that He will be found by us. He is so available, just one conversation away.

Sometimes I would be at work and I would get butterflies in my stomach and hear the Lord say, "I am waiting for you in our room..." It was like the love of my life was waiting for me to spend time with me. I would get home and shut the door and go into that place and just talk to Jesus like I would talk to a best friend. He taught me so much during that time. I was only taught by the Holy Spirit. I did not fit in with my dope friends anymore, and I did not quite fit in with the church crowd yet, so I was in this place of only being taught by the Holy Spirit, and it was beautiful. It was just like Paul—he found himself in an awkward situation when he got saved because he didn't fit in with the people who persecuted the church anymore, but he also did not fit in with the disciples, so he was taught by God.

I was truly a Saul to Paul, and I let the Word of God teach me everything that I know. That was the book that I went to with every issue in life, and it always had the answer. I would go in my room and shut the door and talk to my Father, who was in heaven and heard me and answered me. Does that sound familiar to you? It is Matthew 6:6 (NKJV), "But you, when you pray, go into your room, and when you have shut your door, pray to your Father who is in the secret place; and your Father who sees in secret will reward you openly." See, it is simpler than we think. We read the Bible, and we do what it says. Ha! What a crazy concept! Just read the Bible and do what it says.

I worked at The Popcorn Gallery like it was the Hilton Inn. I mopped those floors until they shined! I would sing every day while I was mopping:

> *Jesus, you are the lover of my soul, Jesus, I will never let you go, you've taken me, from the miry clay, set my feet upon the rock and now I know...I love you and I need you, though my world may fall I'll never let you go.... My Savior, my closest friend, I will worship you until the very end.*

That song was written in my heart because I was in the mud when he found me. He really did take me out of the mud and out of the miry clay. He really did set my feet upon the rock, and I know I love Him, and I can't live without Him. I made candy and popcorn with a smile on my face every day, and I fell in love with everything and everybody. I loved people, I loved babies, and I loved puppy dogs and butterflies and literally everything that came my way. I was so full of Christ and his love for everything.

Lecrae had just released a song called "Tell the World"; it was all about telling the world that you aren't the same person and that you are brand new. I was driving down Highway 80 one day listening to that song, and the Lord dropped it in my heart to get baptized. I thought to myself, *Okay, Lord, if that is You, You will lead me and show me how You want me to do it*. Right then I looked up and saw a big billboard that said "baptism." *Well, okay, Lord*, I thought. *We are doing this*. I went to church at Life Bridge the following Sunday, and guess what announcement they had, "We are doing baptisms next week, and here is how you sign up." I signed up right then and there. I will never forget the day I was baptized. It felt like I could finally show the world what was happening inside of my heart. I really was a new woman; I was not the same. I was honestly a completely different person. Not saying I didn't struggle because I was still a human, but I was a human who had been empowered by the Holy Spirit to never go back to who she was, to die to my old way of life and be born again. Pastor Tom walked over to me, and he said these words, and I have never forgotten them; he said, "Brittney, there is an assignment from hell that has been broken off of your life…" He had no idea, but my favorite verse at that time was "the power of the wicked will be broken" (Psalm 37:17, NIV). That was true—there had been an assignment from hell against me that was broken, and I was so grateful for it, and I am still so grateful for it. If Jesus got baptized, we should get baptized. We should get baptized in the water, but we should also get baptized in the spirit, and I had been baptized in both water and the Holy Spirit that day. It was a beautiful day, and I got out of the water thanking God for bringing me that far. Thanking God for all He had done for me—He had released me from jail and brought my kids back to me just like He said He would. He kept His promises to me—He keeps His promises to me. He is faithful and true.

Chapter 20

GO AND TELL THE OTHERS

> *"And then he told them, 'Go into all the world and preach the Good News to everyone.'"*
>
> Mark 16:15 (NLT)

God restored everything to me. He redeemed everything. I began to seek Him like I never had before, and He did a total miracle of restoration and redemption in my life. He gave me all my children back. He led me to start selling cars to make a living for my family. I remember one night in that prayer room He told me that He wanted me to share my story with other people, so I began to fast and pray about that and start preparing it on paper. Supernaturally, I got invited to give my testimony at Serenity Church in 2016. I had been living for the Lord and sold out for the Lord for two years. I was not married, but I had all my children back, and I was enjoying that.

That night was powerful. I shared my story and had an altar call, and many people responded. There was a boy in the crowd that night who did not want to be there. He was living at a men's program called "House of Disciples"; his buddies had invited him to come watch me speak, and he really wasn't feeling it. He told them he thought he was just going to stay home that night, but for whatever reason, right when they were loading the van up, he changed his mind and said he would like to go.

As he sat there that night listening to me give my testimony about what the Lord did in my life, he said, "God, if You can do that for that girl, You can do it for me," and the Lord whispered to Mitch's heart, "You are going to marry that girl."

Mitch was shocked. *Marry that girl?* he thought. *Man, I must be trippin'*, he said to himself, but he held onto that, and when he got home, he said, "Okay, God, if I am supposed to marry that girl, then You will make a way for it to happen."

One year later, I was asked to come work for Patterson Nissan. Trey Patterson, a wonderful man of God, had seen me give my testimony and invited me to come out and work at a brand-new dealership that he was building. The first day I came to work I saw a man whom I had never met, so I went over to him and introduced myself, "Hi, I'm Brittney Major."

"I know who you are," Mitch responded, which honestly took me off guard because I did not know who he was. "I saw you give your testimony at Serenity last year, and it really inspired me, and I recently got put on staff at House of Disciples, plus I work here full time, and your story really inspired me and gave me hope, so thank you for that."

One year later the Lord did exactly what He told Mitch He was going to do, and we got married. Another promise fulfilled. Little did Mitch know, I had spent time in my prayer room for *years*, saying, "God, I lift my future husband to You. Lord, set him on fire for You and cause our paths to cross. God, redeem him and restore him. If he has lost his children, Lord, bring them home just like You did for me."

One year later, Mitch's son came to live with us, and our family was complete. We were living in the promised land. God had freed us from Egypt. He had delivered us. We will not forget how great and awesome the Lord is.

If my book is in your hands, I want you to know that it is not by accident. The Lord does everything on purpose. If it happens, good or bad, it is on purpose, but even the bad the Lord uses for good. God told me, "Go and tell the others."

I believe the Lord wanted me to write this book to bring you hope. Maybe you are not on drugs, but you have a family member you are believing for the Lord to set free. Maybe it is you who needs to be reminded that the Lord is a promise keeper and a matchmaker. God is not a man that He should lie to you. You need to be reminded of His goodness and His faithfulness. Life happens, and don't get me wrong, a lot of disappointing things have happened in my life even after God changed my life.

I think a lot of people fall for the lies from the devil because they line up with what they can see. That is why the Bible tells us to not walk by sight but to walk by faith. What you see might not look anything like faith; you must focus on what you cannot see. You must focus on *truth* and Jesus in the midst of your storm and in the midst of your heartache. When you stumble, you get back up! That is how we roll. We get knocked down sometimes, but God is with us in every step we take. God's ways and thoughts are higher than ours, so if you are confused on what is happening right now, it could be you need to think higher; you need to focus higher. One thing I know for sure is all of heaven's armies are fighting for you. Lord, I ask You to open our eyes to see all of heaven's armies fighting for us. You are here with us, God; open our eyes to see and open our ears to hear. You are never abandoned, and you are never rejected. You belong to Jesus, and fear can never conquer you because perfect love casts out fear. I pray you get your fight on. I pray you speak to the giant in your life and tell it that you know who you are and you know who your God is. Let faith arise in you! Fight the good faith of faith. Plead the blood of Jesus over your home and your marriage and your children. Do you remember the story in the Old Testament about Passover? *One person* took the blood, put it on the door, and guess what? The whole family on the inside, the whole household, was saved by one person putting blood on the door. Remember that today, you are the one who can plead the blood and break the curses off your household. God is with you, and He is for you. He is in every step you take; you are never alone.

I pray you learn to get out of yourself. Stop complaining and grumbling and get happy about the fact that you are still alive and you are still breathing, and as long as you are breathing, there is hope for you; there is purpose for you. We can get so caught up in grumbling and being snotty and crabby to people. *Stop it*—be grateful for the things you have! Stop wanting what everyone else has—stop wanting to look like the next girl, and just be happy with who God created you to be and who you are!

The last time I checked, there are eight billion people on the planet, and not *one* of them has the same fingerprint as you. You are one of a kind! Be happy that God made you and only made one of you. He has something for you to do. He created you with a purpose. You are the solution to a problem. Don't get down on yourself if you haven't been living right and you haven't been walking in love. Just say "duh" and start today! If the shoe fits, kick it off! You must start somewhere. Begin to glorify God in your heart and thank Him. Thankfulness can get you out of a rut quicker than anything. Glorify the Lord, magnify the Lord, and lift His name up! Cry out to Him, and ask Him to help you. I dare you to start doing what Matthew 6 says and go in your room and shut the door and pray to your Father in heaven and see if you don't start seeing things change. I see irregular things happening on a regular basis because of prayer to my Father, who sees me in private and rewards me.

Just like I have a story, you have a story. You have a unique story about things the Lord has done in your life, and I urge you to go and tell the others. Begin to share with other people the power of God in your own life. Begin to share with others the prayers answered and promises fulfilled in your life. The Bible says you overcome by the blood of the Lamb and the word of your testimony!

One of the most important pieces of advice I can give you is this—forgive everyone, love your enemies, and let Christ's love manifest in you and through you to others. I say, "This is a test, and Daddy is watching" a lot, and what I mean by that is your heart is being tested. Are you okay when things do not go your way? You must be okay when things don't go your way. One of my favorite scriptures is, "I have been crucified with Christ, it is no longer I who live but Christ who lives *in me*" (Galatians 2:20, NIV). Does Christ live *in you*?

If Christ is in you, you do not have to go to church to have church. Christ is in you, working through you everywhere you go. I learned early that God wanted to use me at the gas station and at Walmart and sometimes at church, too, but literally wherever I went.

I remember being in my prayer room one night and saying, "God, I want to *change* the *world*!" and the Lord responded, "You want to change the world?" and I was like, "Yes, I want to be a world changer, and I want to change the world," and I will never forget what He said to me; He said, "Okay, start on Highway 80," and that is exactly what I did. Back then I drove a 2007 Ford Expedition, and I would get in that truck, crank it, and put my hands on the steering wheel and say, "God, lead me wherever You want me to go today, empower me to be a blessing to others, and use me today for Your glory…" And He would tell me, "Turn left here, now go down this road…now take right at this next light…now go down to this intersection…see that lady walking down the street? Minister to her…" It was mind-blowing how God would lead me to people. I used to be off every Tuesday, and that is what I did with my time on Tuesdays. Letting Jesus live in you is *wild* and fun; being led by the Holy Spirit is not boring! It is fun and miraculous, and it ruined my normal life. I have helped a lot of people through those Tuesdays with me and the Lord and Him driving that Ford Expedition through me.

We must learn to hear the voice of the Lord in our everyday lives; it is supposed to be normal, and we must learn to do what He tells us to do.

One night I had a dream. In my dream, I was standing in a strip club, and I walked over to where the music was playing, and I changed the music to worship music, and I started worshiping God in the middle of the strip club, and as I worshiped God, all of the dancers in the club came around me, and they lifted their hands to heaven, and they started worshiping God too—then, boom, I woke up.

Whoa, I must have eaten some pizza before bed to have that wild dream... I thought to myself and kind of laughed at myself, and then I heard the Holy Spirit say, "Go," and I just felt in my heart that I was supposed to go to the strip club in Longview and witness to the girls. I called up Miranda Streed. I said, "Miranda, this is going to sound so crazy, but I had a dream. I went into a strip club, and I was witnessing to some of the girls in there, and I was thinking about going tonight, and I was wondering if you want to come with me. And I was also wondering if you could tell me how many gifts to buy." "Girl, you *know* I am down, and I think about seven would be good for a Friday night; usually there aren't many more than seven girls..."

Miranda was my best friend's little sister, and she had grown up in a Christian home just like my best friend and myself and gone to Christian school and all of the things, but she had gotten caught up in the world and all the world has to offer; she actually worked at a strip club prior to this dream I had, but she didn't work there anymore, and she was coming out of that lifestyle, and she was about to start her life completely over before she was tragically murdered in her own home on April 4th, 2017. That was a terrible day for my best friend and her family. I remember about six months prior my best friend Courtney trying to reach her little sister and get her out of that lifestyle, and she texted me and said, "Brittney, what do I do? How can I reach her?" "Just grab her when you see her next and give her the biggest hug and look her directly in the eyes and tell her how much you love her..." And that is exactly what Courtney did. She looked her sister in the eyes and hugged her and said, "I love you so much," and it wasn't very long after that someone took her life.

I walked in the mall thinking to myself, *I cannot believe I am about to walk into a strip club tonight...* I laughed to myself as I walked around picking out body lotion and candles and little gifts for them. After I bought gifts, I went to Dollar General and bought gift bags and a ten-pack of cards. I wrote on each of the cards a letter from

God. I just let the Lord lead me on that. I let Him sort of say what He wanted to say, what was on His heart. I remember writing that "you are beautiful, and I love you, and I can fulfill you," and on one of the cards, I even wrote, "Will you marry me?" at the end of it. I felt like this person had been wanting someone to be married to, and she was especially broken and lonely. After I was done with the cards, I called my mom and one of my closest friends, Jacqueline, to come with me, and they both said they would, so there we went on a Friday night, off to the strip club.

My heart was pounding when we pulled into the parking lot. It was still light outside but barely, and the sun was beginning to set. I turned around and looked at my best friend, who was seven months pregnant at the time, and I said, "Girl, I do not know what I was thinking. You cannot go in here; it is a bar, and there is a lot of cigarette smoke and stuff, so how about I go in? And you and Mom can sit in the car and wait for me to get out." My mom was as radical as I was. Matter of fact, I got it from her! I was not worried about her at all, but she agreed to sit in the car with Jaqueline. I got all the gifts out of the back of my car, and I started on my way to the front door of the strip club.

When I first walked in, I got some crazy looks. "Ummm, hi, I know this sounds crazy, but I had a dream that I was in this place, and then I felt like God told me to come and to bring some gifts for the girls to just give them and pray for them before they go on stage tonight. Would that be okay?" I said to the man staring a hole in me. "What church are you with?" he snapped at me. "Well, I am not really with a church. I am just a Christian, and I love Jesus, and I just feel like this is what He wanted me to do," I said back. "Yeah, you can go back there. The girls are just starting to get ready. Just go bang on that door in the back, and Angelica will let you in..." he said.

"Bang, bang, bang, Angelica?" I asked as I knocked on the door. "Yeah, who are you?" she asked. "My name is Brittney, and I know this sounds crazy, but I had a dream that I was here last night, and I just felt like God wanted me to come here and bring you and the girls gifts and pray for you and love on you and encourage you before you go on stage tonight..." I started walking the room and handing each girl who was getting ready that night a gift, introducing myself to them, and praying for them. They were so precious; they were so open to what God was doing in the moment. Their hearts were tender, and they were not mean at all to me. As I got ready to leave, and I was about to walk out the door, one of them came running up behind me... "Brittney?" she asked. "Yes," I said as I turned around toward her. "Will you pray for me and my boyfriend before you leave? He is over there at the bar, and we could really use your prayers. We are going through a lot right now..." So that is what I did. I turned around, met him, and prayed for them, and I could not help but be emotional as I got back to the car to tell the story of what had happened to Jaqueline and my mom. Wow, what if I did not obey? What if I just shrugged it off as just a dream and not a big deal? What if I did not show up for these girls? Thank You, Lord. I am sensitive to what You are saying, and I do things even though they seem crazy. Thank You for helping me and leading me. God's leadership is perfect. He has such a heart and such compassion for people. He loved those girls, and He wanted them to each feel special and loved that night. Miranda did not make it that night because her boyfriend had her car, and I never got to speak to Miranda again after that night because her life was taken. But I know she wanted to be there with me, and she helped me get my foot in the door, and she helped me orchestrate the gifts, and I am so thankful for her.

    I went from working at The Popcorn Gallery to working at a Japanese restaurant to working at a car dealership. One day I was at the car dealership, and a man came in wanting to go on a test drive. He was an older man with gray, scruffy hair and a silver beard. He wanted to test drive a Frontier, so just like any good car salesperson,

I grabbed the keys so we could take one on a spin. I pulled up to the front of the dealership, and he got on the driver's side. I got in the passenger's side, and we took off. While he was driving, I noticed this growth coming out of his neck. I felt like the Holy Spirit told me to ask him what it was. I said, "Sir, I don't want to weird you out or anything, but I have this thing where I hear God speak to me, and if you don't mind me asking, what is that growth on your neck?"

"It's cancer. I am eaten up with it. My thirty-three-year-old daughter just died from it; my wife had it; it's all in my family...cancer has killed a lot of us, and I am sure I will be next." The Holy Spirit told me, "Pray for him." So I was like, "Is it okay if I pray for you?" "Well, let me pull the car over," he responded to me. He pulled the car over, and I just laid my hand on his neck, and I started praying for him. I prayed that cancer would be broken and that his bloodline would have no more cancer in Jesus' name. The man was crying, and he said, "The only thing I know about God is an old hymn from when my grandma used to take me to church when I was little." I told him that he could know God just like I know God, and I asked him if he wanted that, and he said yes. So he let me lead him in a prayer and got saved on that test drive in that Frontier. He asked Jesus to be the Lord of his life. He was crying, and I was crying. He did not buy the truck that day, but he got all he ever needed. A few days later, he came back to Nissan and told me he just wanted to thank me again for praying for him that day and how his life was changing, and he was so grateful for me. What if I did not listen? What if I just went on casually about my day in selfishness like life is about me? My wants? My needs? And I wasn't sensitive to the voice of the Lord?

There was another night I was ministering to some girls at a ministry, and the Lord told me to go up to one of them and say, "God is going to return that baby back to you." I had no idea who she was; she was a young, pretty girl, and I had never seen her before. I asked her if I could pray for her, and I said exactly what the Lord told me to say, "God is going to restore that baby back to you." She started weeping, and she told me she had just lost her baby to methamphetamine use. She said her newborn baby tested positive, and CPS took her. After that prayer meeting, she decided that God was real, and He had spoken to her through me, and she worked that program and graduated and got her baby back! She still has that child to this day. God is so good. Restoring babies to parents, bringing children home from afar.

The last story I will leave you with is the most recent story. I went to Dollar Tree to pick up some stuff for my kid's birthday. I needed some gift bags and stuffing, ten dollars' worth of stuff. I went in and picked out what I needed, and while I was in line, I heard the Lord say, "Pay for this lady in front of you." I had no idea how much money I had in my account, but I knew it wasn't much, so I was like, "Are You sure, Lord?" and I was like, "If that is You, give me a sign…" Right when I asked for a sign, her card declined, and she was fishing another card out of her wallet…

"Excuse me, ma'am. I don't want to weird you out or anything, but I have this thing where I hear the Lord speaking sometimes, and I think He wants me to pay for your stuff today." As I was talking, I just swiped my card and paid for all her stuff. It was a lot of food, groceries, and stuff. She started crying and said, "Thank you so much; thank you; thank you." I said, "Sure, no problem. God loves you…" She left, and I went ahead and checked out. I was walking to the car, and I noticed the lady and her friend were waiting for me in the parking lot. "Ma'am, can we talk to you for just a minute?" "Sure," I said. "There is no way you could have known this, but I have been in a deep depression for about three weeks. It has been so bad I have not even gotten out of bed except to go to the bathroom for three full weeks, and my friend made me get out of bed today and come to Dollar Tree to get food and stuff for my house, and you did that. You paid for my stuff, and you told me God loved me, and you have restored my faith in humanity and made me realize today that not all people are bad, and matter of fact, there are some people who are good. Thank you." Even though that lady had been in a dark place, the Lord saw her in her bed, depressed, and used me as a vessel to minister to her and to bring her some hope and love. He sees us in a crowd of ten thousand people; He sees you, and He understands you. He understands your weakness, and He sympathizes with you and has compassion for you.

Before I ever did ministry on a stage, I did ministry in a strip club, in Walmart, on a street corner. Some people don't agree with the way I do ministry, but I am not concerned with it. At least I am out here trying. So many Christians just stay so safe, and they never get out of the boat! They just sit in the boat with a seat belt on and never even try to get out in the trenches and introduce people to Jesus. When Jesus revealed Himself to me, I knew it was my mandate to lead people to Him, to show them a way out of the darkness and out of the trap of the enemy. His word is a lamp unto our feet. Without that lamp, we are in the dark, and we stumble. With that lamp we can see where we are going. We are also the light of the world; we are supposed to shine bright and show people what true freedom looks like. I would challenge you with this question. Are you shining your light bright for all men to see? Are you getting out of the boat and out of your comfort zone to bring hope to the hopeless? If you aren't, that's okay; you can start today.

Chapter 21

JESUS OVER EVERYTHING

Christ is the exact likeness of the unseen God. He existed before God made anything at all, and, in fact, Christ himself is the Creator who made everything in heaven and earth, the things we can see and the things we can't; the spirit world with its kings and kingdoms, its rulers and authorities; all were made by Christ for his own use and glory. He was before all else began and it is his power that holds everything together. He is the Head of the body made up of his people—that is, his Church— which he began; and he is the Leader of all those who arise from the dead, so that he is first in everything; for God wanted all of himself to be in his Son.

Colossians 1:15–19 (TLB)

I love superhero movies. Probably my all-time favorite one is Marvel's *Avengers: Endgame*. There is a scene in that movie where Dr. Strange travels into the future to see if they can win the war against Thanos. When he returns, he says, "There are fourteen million six hundred and five outcomes to this." And Iron Man asks him, "How many do we win?" and Dr. Strange says, "One." Iron Man dying was the only way the superheroes could go on to claim the victory. The odds were completely stacked against them, but there was *one* way to win. I want you to know the same thing is true for you. The odds can be stacked against you, and it can look like there are fourteen million different ways for you to lose, but there is *one* way to win, and that way is Jesus. Jesus died so you could win. The victory is yours. He is a statistic-shattering Savior.

"If Christ be anything, He must be everything" (Charles Spurgeon). Jesus is real; the gospel is not a fairytale. You can know Him as your Savior. You can know Him as your Father. You can know Him as your healer. You can know Him as your deliverer. You can know Him as your best friend. He wants to be all of that for you. He wants to speak to you and use you the same way He uses me. He wants to give you words for your family and for your friends and for strangers at the dollar store. He wants to take you on a wild, crazy adventure where you and He partner up and you do things like change the world. You do it for Him, you honor Him, and you give Him all the glory, and guess what? He honors you. You seek Him in private, and He brings you out in front of the public. The way up is always down. I encourage you to give your life to Jesus. Let Him change your life. You may be far from perfect, but the cross says you are worth it. Your heart is still beating, and He is not finished with you. Give Him every part of you until all of you is gone—less of you and more of Him. You are priceless. You are irreplaceable. God is madly in love with you. You are worth the blood of Jesus. He was thinking of you that day He died. He saw you with every wrong made right by His blood. You cannot outrun God. There is nowhere you can go to escape His Spirit. King David said, "If I ascend into heaven, You are there; If I make my bed in hell, behold, You are there" (Psalm 139:8, NKJV). If you are hungry and thirsty and you have done all you can do, go to Jesus. He is a river in the wasteland. He will fill you up inside. Life cuts so deep sometimes, but you are not alone. Scars are part of life. They come with it. It does not matter who you are; you are not exempt from battle scars, but the glory of God can heal our wounded souls and make us whole again. The Holy Spirit is our helper while here on this earth. Jesus said that He had to go away so He could send the Holy Spirit and the Holy Spirit would lead us into all truth and tell us of things to come. The Holy Spirit comforts us, and He speaks to us and reminds us who we are. He leads us, and He guides us. Jesus is in heaven seated at the right hand of God, but the Holy Spirit is here, and He is who helps us while we navigate the rough waters of life. I have the Holy Spirit tattooed on my left wrist. I wanted to be marked by Him. I wanted to look down and see that as a reminder that Jesus will never leave me or forsake me and He sent His Spirit to prove it. He did not leave me to walk alone, but He gave me His Spirit.

I had a vision for this book being twenty-one chapters because I have been arrested twenty-one times. I hope it gave you some idea of the hopeless case that I was and how Jesus turned it all around. Jesus does not require but one thing: everything. You have a choice to make; you can choose to live a normal life and chase after the American dream and make a lot of money, have a farmhouse, a trophy spouse, a boat, and a labradoodle. That American dream will make you so happy for a fleeting time. It will satisfy you until the storms of life hit—then the only thing that matters is what you are anchored to. Christ is our firm foundation. A solid rock that we can stand on, and when the winds of life come and the storm rages on...you can stand. You will not be shaken. You must learn to put Jesus over everything. I am sold out. I am addicted to the Most High. I am standing on a firm foundation and ruining the devil's goods every time I get the chance. There have been many challenges in my life since I converted. I had a battle with skin cancer; I had to have some tests done on my muscles because some doctors thought I had a muscle deterioration disease. Praise God that I did not. My father passed away, and my husband and I had a difficult first three years of marriage. There have been many challenges along the way, but I never lose hope. I never stop trusting that God knows best, and I am right in the center of His will. I honor God through every disappointment. The Bible says, "Do not be afraid of those who kill the body but cannot kill the soul. Rather, be afraid of the One who can destroy both soul and body in hell" (Matthew 10:28, NIV).

I mentioned a little earlier in the book, "This is a test, and Daddy is watching." I promise you that you will be tested along the way of your Christian journey. In Genesis 22 the Bible tells us that "God *test* Abraham." I have had people tell me in the past, "Oh no,

Brittney, God never tests us..." That is false. God, indeed, does test us. The Bible says that God will never tempt us, not test us. There is a difference between the two. God will test you. When I was working in the restaurant industry when I first got out of jail, I had been clean for a couple of years, and I was cleaning up one night after a late shift, and I was sweeping the floor; as I was reaching with the long broom under the table, I accidentally swept up a contact case. I picked up the case and unscrewed the top of it, and it was full of pills. The same kind of pills that I used to take! I was blown away. The left side was full of a certain type of pill I used to take, and the right side was full as well to the end! It was a huge test of my heart! I put that contact case in my apron, and I started my way to the bathroom to flush those pills. I remember when I got to the bathroom, I started making declarations as I flushed those pills. I was saying, "The power of the wicked is broken off of me." That is one of my favorite scriptures to stand on. It is a good one for anyone who has ever come out of addiction. Addiction is a power the devil uses, and we must declare that power is broken off of us. I flushed those pills right down the toilet that day.

I have flushed dope down the toilet that I found at that same restaurant. The devil has tried to get me to go back to my old life so many times, but my mind is made up, my face is set like flint, and I am never going back. I am unashamed; I am all in. The mind is a powerful thing. When we surrender our entire mind, body, and soul to the Lord and when we, for real, lay our lives down at His feet and surrender all, then we can pass the test that God sets before us. I often think about when God tested Abraham that day—what that must have been like for God to ask you to sacrifice your son. Talk about all in—all God did in my case was ask me to flush some stuff and to walk into strip clubs and witness to people and to pay for some groceries. To be able to sacrifice your son—just the willingness and the openness to do that blows my mind. Isn't it beautiful that God asked him to do it, but He did not require it in the end? He provided a ram instead. My question to you is: Are you all in? If you were tested today, your heart was tested; how would you respond? And it is okay if you do not pass every test. I certainly have not passed every test. There have been days I was walking through Walmart picking up dinner on my way home from work, and I was tired, and I had to cook and clean and bathe all the kids and do all the things when I got home, and I felt that nudge from the Holy Spirit, and I didn't do it, but as soon as I got in the car, I was quick to repent, and I told the Lord I was sorry for not obeying. You are not going to get it right every time, but you should try to. You should posture your heart in a way that is all in. His leadership is brilliant, and it would blow your mind the ways He can provide for you and take care of you just by following His leadership. You would be surprised at the things that can be broken off by your obedience. You would be surprised by how the Holy Spirit can do things. When He has His way, things break. When we surrender all, things break. When we let go of pride and offense and selfishness and bitterness, things break off us.

I am not proud of the things I have done. I am embarrassed of it. There is no glory in my story for me. All the glory goes to the Lord for what He did with the broken mess that I made. I made a mess of my life, and He turned it into something beautiful. He redeemed me, and He restored me and gave me a new life. I have had people ask me, "Brittney, if you could go back and do it over again, would you?" The answer to that is yes, but I know that I can't, but if I could do one thing differently, I would have sold out to Jesus as a teenager. I would have gotten on fire for God way sooner than I did. I am in love with Jesus. I wish I would have fallen in love so much sooner. I have been captivated by Him; His love is so strong for us. I was so far gone, so broken, the most hopeless of all cases, and He ran after me. He crashed down all the walls that separated me from Him, and He gave me all I ever needed. Jesus. He is worthy. He is holy. My prayer for you is that He restores your hunger and thirst for Him. The Bible says, "Blessed are those who hunger and thirst for righteousness for they shall be filled" (Matthew 5:6, NIV). I pray that you put this book down and go into your room and shut the door and have a face-to-face encounter with Jesus. You need a fresh face-to-face with Him. When was the last time you had one? When was the last time you made time for the Lord? I pray He brings back your fire. I pray this book has fanned the flame and caused you to think you want to be on fire again! It will not cost you much—just your life. What an honor to get to be with Him! I encourage you to pledge your life to Him! Give Him your all. Be a living sacrifice for Him, and put yourself on the altar! You provide the sacrifice, and let Him provide the fire, and get on fire for Him. He will keep you burning. He is faithful and true. You can trust Him. In a world that seems crazy and chaotic, you can trust Him. I would like to end this book with a prayer. I would love it if you said it with me. You can just take a moment, take a few breaths, and just pray this prayer out loud with me.

Prayer:

Jesus, I want to have a fresh, face-to-face encounter with You right now. I want to be on fire for You. I want to burn for You. I want the real thing. I want to hear Your voice, and I want to obey You at all costs. I honor You, and I invite You into my life and my situation right now. My heart desires You. My soul longs for You. I open my heart to You right now. I fling wide the doors of my chest, and I ask You to make Your home inside of me. Fill me up, God. I lay my life down to You. I am all in, God. I set my face like flint, and I make up my mind right now—there is no going back. Keep me burning with the flame of love. I empty myself right now; I know the only way to get full is to get empty first. I empty myself of pride, bitterness, and unforgiveness, and I make room for You, Holy Spirit. I open my heart to You—have Your way in me, whatever You want to do, whatever

You want to say. God, let me feel Your forgiveness and Your love all around me and Your Spirit living in me. Help me to let go of the past. Help me to let go of all the trauma and abuse that I have gone through. Let Your glory heal every soul wound. Father me, Lord—adopt me today and welcome me into the family of God and into the kingdom of God. Give me passion in my heart and hope in my veins. Help me to burn bright for You, Jesus. I am all in.

> *How thankful I am to Christ Jesus our Lord for choosing me as one of his messengers and giving me the strength to be faithful to him, even though I used to scoff at the name of Christ. I hunted down his people, harming them in every way I could. But God had mercy on me because I didn't know what I was doing, for I didn't know Christ at that time. Oh, how kind our Lord was, for he showed me how to trust him and become full of the love of Christ Jesus. How true it is, and how I long that everyone should know it, that Christ Jesus came into the world to save sinners—and I was the greatest of them all.*
>
> 1 Timothy 1:12–15 (TLB)

About the Author

Brittney Singleton is passionate about the world knowing that Jesus is real and the gospel is not a fairy tale. She was born and raised in Longview, Texas. She married Mitch Singleton on July 21, 2018. They have four children: Madisyn, Connor, Maci, and Maverick. She is an author, evangelist, and public speaker. She loves working with broken people and mentoring drug addicts. She enjoys introducing people to a new way of life, a relationship with Jesus. Her ministry started in 2013. She was a drug addict and career criminal who had been arrested twenty-one times and convicted of several felonies. She had lost all hope for her life and future. She had lost her mind and found herself in a scary world where she could trust no one. She had been raised in church. She gave her heart to Jesus at the age of thirteen, but she was living a prodigal lifestyle. Prodigal means "unrestrained" with no boundaries. On December 31st, 2013, she cried out to God in a cold jail cell. She asked Him to come into her heart and save her and make her a different person. As soon as she prayed that prayer, God came running. He met her in that jail cell. He baptized her with the Holy Spirit and fire. Brittney never looked back. She enjoys carrying this message of hope all over Texas. She speaks at ministries, jails, prisons, and churches. She loves to tell her story of how God runs...

> *"So, he returned home to his father. And while he was still a long distance away, his father saw him coming, and was filled with loving pity and ran and embraced him and kissed him."*
>
> Luke 15:20 (TLB)

Milton Keynes UK
Ingram Content Group UK Ltd.
UKHW010235111224
452348UK00011B/783